TO BE CLEAR

Also by Philip Collins

Start Again: How We Can Fix Our Broken Politics
The Art of Speeches and Presentations
When They Go Low, We Go High

PHILIP COLLINS

TO BE CLEAR

A STYLE GUIDE FOR BUSINESS WRITING

Quercus

First published in Great Britain in 2021 by Quercus.

Quercus Editions Ltd
Carmelite House
50 Victoria Embankment
London EC4Y 0DZ

An Hachette UK company

A CIP catalogue record for this book is available
from the British Library
HB ISBN 978 1 52941 498 1
Ebook ISBN 978 1 52941 499 8

10 9 8 7 6 5 4 3 2 1

Typeset by CC Book Production
Printed and bound in Great Britain by Clays Ltd, Elcograf S.p.A.

Papers used by Quercus are from well-managed forests and other responsible sources.

Contents

'I see but one rule: to be clear. If I am not clear all my world crumbles to nothing.'

Marie-Henri Beyle, 'Stendhal'
A letter to Honoré de Balzac, 30 October 1840

For first you write a sentence
And then you chop it small:
Then mix the bits, and sort them out
Just as they chance to fall:
The order of the phrases
Makes no difference at all.

Lewis Carroll, *Poeta Fit, Non Nascitur*

PART ONE

The Virtue of Clarity

The Red Thread

The purpose of this book is to help business executives write clearly and meaningfully. So much writing for business fails this elementary test. That is why this book is a rallying cry for better writing as well as a guide to how it might be done. If, after reading this text and referring to the dictionary it provides, nobody ever again writes 'we will launch a red-thread concept across a range of buzz-worthy physical and digital touchpoints' when all they mean is that they will give you an idea you can use in all your business communication, then its purpose will have been served.

The best idea you will ever be given, the best red-thread concept of the lot, is to be as simple, as precise and as brief as you can, consistent with saying all of what you mean and not a word more, or indeed less. My advice throughout is to heed Stendhal who put a credo for writing into a letter to Balzac in October 1840: 'I see but one rule: to be clear. If I am not clear all my world crumbles to nothing.'

The virtue of clarity does not derive from a fastidious obsession with language. You will find little pedantry in this dictionary. I lay down no rules. I offer instead advice on techniques that work well and distinguish them from techniques which do not work so well. This is not one of those style guides which is filled with fussy strictures on grammar or pompous instruction on punctuation. You do not need any instruction on grammar, a discipline in which you have been accomplished since you were at least two years of age. Most readers will not be able to distinguish between the use of stative and non-stative verbs with a present participle. Yet we do this in practice, in conversation, perfectly well and have been doing it ever since we first learned to speak.

Neither should a language be set in aspic. Change is not evidence of decline. Sticklers and pedants have been making this bogus claim ever since William Caxton lamented in 1475 that the upshot of his inventing the printing press was that 'our language now used veryeth from what whiche was used and spoken when I was borne'. Change and invention is, in fact, the lifeblood of a thriving language.

The virtue we should serve is clarity because if you are not clear what you are saying, it invariably follows that you are not clear what you are doing and if you are not clear what you are doing, your world crumbles to nothing.

Business is a simple enterprise made complex by people who do it badly. The typical corporate strategy is a convoluted document of faulty thinking. A murky piece of writing is always the tip-off that a company is not clear what it is doing. It is never difficult to be clear about a good idea. Thinking and writing are a single process and clarity of expression needs to be built in from the start. 'If a man does not know which port he is steering to, no wind is favourable', said Seneca the Younger and nobody who disdains this advice will write well. Business executives who do listen, though, will not only talk less nonsense, they will make fewer errors because the errors they make will be plain and evident, even to themselves.

Straight Thinking

This is an ancient insight. If Aristotle were rewriting his *The Art of Rhetoric* today for a corporate audience, he could increase sales while doing no violence to the argument if he called the book *The Art of Strategy*. Delete the word 'rhetoric' throughout and substitute for it the word 'strategy' and *The Art of Rhetoric* would become the best manual for corporate success on the market. That is because Aristotle's use of the term 'rhetoric' is not confined to verbal expression. *The Art of Rhetoric* – and this applies to Cicero's *De oratore* and Quintilian's *Institutio Oratoria* too – is a primer in the fact that straight talking relies on straight thinking.

Aristotle defines rhetoric as 'the ability in any particular case to see the available means of persuasion'. A good business is an unbroken series of successful acts of persuasion; to understand the market; to inspire employees to give of their best; to entice potential clients or customers to purchase your goods. In a rivalrous market, the prize goes to the company that mounts the most persuasive series of arguments. Corporate strategy is simply a modern description of the way a company defines its acts of persuasion. It might therefore make sense to seek the counsel of the ancient experts.

The three branches of oratory that Aristotle describes in *The Art of Rhetoric* are useful business categories. He names them deliberative, forensic and display and each branch applies to a different setting and uses a different time signature. Each category is an act of persuasion and each one demands a verdict from the listening public. All three types of oratory are both familiar and necessary in contemporary business. If we take them together, then Aristotle's thought provides a method for clear strategic thought which will lead to plain and comprehensible writing.

Forensic rhetoric was originally the judicial language of court. The forensic speaker is concerned with time past and is determined to establish the facts of the matter. Forensic rhetoric deals, writes Aristotle, with 'accusation and defence' and 'requires the consideration of (1) the motives of wrongdoing; (2) the frame of mind of the wrongdoer; (3) the kind of people to whom he does wrong'. Forensic rhetoric is the language of charge and accusation, of exoneration and conviction, none of which is a stranger to the world of competitive business.

For example, on 10 April 2018 Mark Zuckerberg testified before the United States Senate Commerce and Judiciary Committees. Zuckerberg had been summoned to discuss Russian interference in the 2016 presidential election and the use of data provided by users of Facebook. Over the course of 600 questions from 100 lawmakers, Zuckerberg relied, whether he knew it or not, on the techniques of forensic rhetoric. He opened by conceding some of Facebook's failures and then went on to suggest how those errors might be rectified: 'It's not enough to just give people a voice. We need to make sure that people aren't using it to harm other people or to spread misinformation.'

Aristotle's second category is display, which is rhetoric put up on stage. The rhetoric of display takes place in the present. Its subject is, as Aristotle writes in the *Rhetoric*, 'praise or censure, the objects of which are the noble and the disgraceful, virtue and vice'.

Steve Jobs delivered an uplifting display address to Stanford University graduates in 2005. The convention of these commencement speeches is to offer maxims of advice, drawn from the speaker's dramatic autobiography, for the graduating cohort. After a moving description of being told that he should prepare for death from pancreatic cancer (which, mercifully, subsequently proved to be curable), Jobs poured flattery on his audience and, with his characteristic excess of schmaltz, asked them to summon their own inner wisdom: 'Don't let the noise of others' opinions drown out your own inner voice. And most important, have the courage to follow your heart and intuition. They somehow already know what you truly want to become.'

Deliberative rhetoric, Aristotle's third branch of oratory, applies to the realm of action. 'We deliberate', writes Aristotle, 'about matters that seem to admit of two possibilities.' This was originally intended to apply to the assembly in Athens in which the deliberative speaker refines an argument to clarify both the advantages of his preferred course and the pitfalls of alternative options. The purview of the deliberative speaker lies in the future, with the hope that his listeners be stirred to action.

In 2015, Bill Gates gave a fine example of deliberative rhetoric in a TED talk prophetically entitled *We're Not Ready*. Gates argued that the world is unprepared for the outbreak of a pandemic in which the virus spreads through the air, rather like the Spanish flu of 1918. His case sounded at the time provocatively unlikely: 'So here's what would happen. It would spread throughout the world very, very quickly. And you can see there's over 30 million people die from that epidemic. So this is a serious problem.' After setting out the problem, Gates deliberated on the possible responses. He pointed out that stronger health systems were needed in poor countries and so was investment in vaccines and diagnostics. The cost of preparing, he concluded, would be a small fraction of failing to prepare.

The three branches of oratory, the combined rhetorical effects of Zuckerberg, Jobs and Gates, together create a method that yields clear strategic thought.

The first step is to deliberate. Good thinking requires research, discussion and consultation with experts. The purpose is to refine the central argument. Then, when a clear statement of intent has been adduced, the argument needs to be put to a forensic test. Every weakness, factual and conceptual, needs to be interrogated by sceptics until all its flaws are identified and eradicated. An argument that has survived this questioning will have a strong internal core. It may not yet, however, be displayed to best effect so attention must be then paid, in the third and final part of the process, to the manner in which the case is expressed.

This method – deliberate, interrogate, display – will produce a text which has been considered and tested and which will therefore be vivid and clear. Isocrates, the sophist who did a great deal to popularize the idea that rhetoric was a teachable skill, used to package his insights up as a pamphlet, delivered in lieu of a spoken address. In the corporate boardroom, the product will be a clear and well-written strategy paper.

Magical Things

Business writing was once crisp, clear and close to the tone and rhythm of common language. Take this example from Benjamin Seebohm Rowntree's *The Human Factor in Business*, published in 1921:

> That is why I have written this book, which largely consists of a description of the way in which the directors of the Cocoa Works, York, have tried to solve some of the human problems of business administration. I deal with

the subject under five heads - Wages, Hours, Economic Security of the Workers, Working Conditions, Joint Control, - and in each section I indicate the end we have in view, the means by which we try to achieve it, and the extent of our success. I should be the last to claim any special merit for our methods, but we have received so much help from others, that it seemed incumbent on us to throw our experience into the common stock of knowledge, in the hope that we may thus repay, in some measure, the debt we owe to the experience of other firms.

Rowntree goes on to write elegantly about the set of public obligations the company owes to public authorities. The generosity exhibited in this passage lasts the length of the book. The prose throughout is clear and plain and Rowntree uses no words that would not be easily comprehensible to a member of the lay public.

Somewhere during the century from 1921 until now something went badly wrong. Examples of poor writing are legion today but here is one specimen, chosen not to pour scorn on the celebrity speaker but simply because the passage is, sadly, so typical. In 2015, Satya Nadella, the Chief Executive Officer at Microsoft, addressed his employees with the following:

Team, I believe that we can do magical things when we come together with a shared mission, clear strategy, and a culture that brings out the best in us individually and collectively. Last week I shared how we are aligning our structure to our strategy. Today, I want to share more on the overall context and connective tissue between our mission, worldview, strategy and culture. It is critical that we start the new fiscal year with this shared vision on what we can do and who we want to become. Every great company has an enduring mission. Our mission is to empower every person and every organization on the planet to achieve more. I'm proud to share that this is our new official mission statement. This mission is ambitious and at the core of what our customers deeply care about. We have unique capability in harmonizing the needs of both individuals and organizations. This is in our DNA. We also deeply care about taking things global and making a difference in lives and organizations in all corners of the planet . . .

It is hard to know where to start with this, although it is clear enough where to stop, which is at the beginning with the word 'team'. Note, in the first sentence, how unclear Nadella makes the attribution of causation. The unspecified 'magical things' derive from a collection of other virtues – coming together with a shared mission, a clear strategy and a culture that brings out the best in everyone. Yet these causal factors are all themselves complex virtues which cannot be simply assumed into life, as they are in this passage.

If this sentence means anything at all, it means only that, once you have assembled all the factors that lead to success, then success is assured. It is a tautology stretched to inordinate length. There is no serious attempt to weight the relative causal importance of these factors or to specify how they align to the strategy (whatever that means). Lost in a blizzard of truisms, we cannot see a thing. As soon as we decipher what Mr Nadella is saying we find that he is not saying anything.

Having opened with empty claims, Mr Nadella then pulls the focus back to 'the overall context', a vast landscape which, strangely for something that sounds so important, only shares the same billing within the sentence as 'the connective tissue' between the mission, the worldview, the strategy and the culture. We have no way of knowing what 'the connective tissue' refers to. He probably means no more than that the strategy, the worldview, the mission and the culture are connected, which is a rather commonplace observation. Or perhaps they are not yet connected but need to be. Note, too, how a 'worldview' is suddenly smuggled in, as if we didn't already have enough to think about. A worldview surely precedes a mission, a strategy and a culture and informs all three. Not here, where it is relegated to the same status in a list of four.

This is bad enough but, sadly, the worst is still to come. The definition of the mission, when it arrives, is so absurdly inflated that it would make a cat laugh. The mission is to empower every person and every organization on the planet to achieve more. Every person, no matter what their passion – Benedictine monks, repertory actors doing Shakespeare, the company that has the cleaning contract for Birmingham city council, a retired crofter on Jura – there is not one of them that will not find their capacity to live the good life enhanced by Microsoft. We then learn that the source of this ambition, which vaults over grandeur into lunacy, is Microsoft's customers. They care about more than being rendered a good service, apparently. They care deeply about helping everyone on the planet.

Then, at the end of this passage, Mr Nadella capriciously changes the subject. Leaving his string of indecipherable and unlikely claims undeveloped, he asserts that 'we' (who? the company? its customers? everyone on the planet?) have a unique capability to harmonize the needs of individuals and companies. Even if we allow that this is a real task (which it isn't), by what warrant can he claim that his people (whoever they are) have a unique capability in this regard? It is no good enlisting an ailing metaphor to claim that this is in our DNA. Just for good measure, we then veer off in another direction altogether, to tick off the obligatory word 'global'. We have had no story, no person, no example and no sense. At no point does Mr Nadella make a concrete point. He goes on in this vein for more than 1,500 words and it is all just high-sounding nothing.

Well, almost all of it is nothing. In fact, Mr Nadella does smuggle in a meaningful statement, suitably surrounded by empty optimism and subtly shrouded in mystery. See if you can spot it in the next passage: 'I believe that culture is not static. It evolves every day based on the behaviors of everyone in the organization. We are in an incredible position to seize new growth this year. We will need to innovate in new areas, execute against our plans, make some tough choices in areas where things are not working and solve hard problems in ways that drive customer value. I really do believe that we can achieve magical things when we come together as one team and focus.' Now we see that the magical things will not necessarily involve all the team. There will be some tough choices to be made in areas where things are not working. This is likely to be the one sentence that resonated.

It is easy to believe that the word 'pidgin' is thought to be a Chinese rendering of the English word 'business'. This is what George Orwell meant when he said a bad writer is 'like a cuttlefish squirting out ink'. Writing of this type is now ubiquitous in the business world. People in modern business who write and speak like Seebohm Rowntree are decidedly rare. But Rowntree's exemplary clarity shows that business language has not always been terrible and need not be now. So where did it all go wrong? What was the impulse for executives to cease talking like Seebohm Rowntree and start talking like Satya Nadella?

The Discipline of Business

The pivotal changes took place in the early decades of the twentieth century. This was an era in which life became greatly more involved and complex. In the academy and in the conduct of business itself the response to complexity was increasing specialization. The professions began to develop their own ways of talking and that specialization came to be described in private language.

The story of what went wrong has three lead players. The first is a man who won the American Open tennis doubles championship and just missed out on a bronze medal in golf at the 1900 Olympics. The second is a man who, in his day, fancied himself as America's proto-fascist President. But the place to start is with the third player, the most famous film star of the 1930s. Charlie Chaplin's last silent film, *Modern Times*, released in 1936, is the perfect statement of a new regime of capitalist specialization. *Modern Times* is also the final outing for Chaplin's favourite character, Little Tramp, whom we encounter on an assembly line, screwing nuts at a velocity comically beyond his capacity. The pace and tedium of work on the production line give Little Tramp a nervous break-down. After a chain of improbable accidents, Little Tramp is imprisoned and, when he is offered release, maintains that he would rather stay in jail than return to the factory.

The target of *Modern Times* is Frederick Winslow Taylor, the curator of the mechanized wilderness. Taylor was a talented man. A junior tennis and golf prodigy, he became the original guru of management consultancy. When he was working as a machinist at the Midvale Steel Works in Philadelphia, Taylor noticed that the workers were not fully active at their machines. He began to wonder at the cost and the upshot of his obser-vations was a guidebook for efficient work, *The Principles of Scientific Management* (1911). In this book Taylor adduced the four principles of optimal efficiency:

1. Replace rule-of-thumb work methods with methods based on a scientific study of the tasks.

2. Scientifically select, train, and develop each employee rather than passively leaving them to train themselves.
3. Provide detailed instruction and supervision of each worker in the performance of that worker's discrete task.
4. Divide work nearly equally between managers and workers, so that the managers apply scientific management principles to planning the work and the workers actually perform the tasks.

Factories run on these lines demanded total standardization, invigilated and enforced by officious managers. Workers were set against the clock and output was tracked and charted. Taylor was so obsessively rigorous that he claimed to have calculated formulae for the most efficient use of a shovel, the best way to move iron pigs in a steel mill and the quickest procedure for the manual inspection of ball bearings.

The scientific basis of Taylor's calculations was dubious, to say the least. When Taylor was brought into the Bethlehem Steel Company in Pennsylvania he decreed that 'a first class man' could load pig iron at a rate of 47.5 tons a day, rather than the 12.5 tons a day that was the average. Though he liked to stand around, stopwatch in hand, to give the impression of mathematical precision, Taylor had come to his figure of 47.5 tons a day by observing a band of powerful Hungarians for an hour. He took the output of the best of them, rounded it up, took off a made-up percentage for rest and arrived at his conclusion that a first-rate worker could load pig iron at a rate of 47.5 tons a day. Summoned to Congress in January 1912 to testify before a House Committee to Investigate Taylor and Other Systems of Shop Management, Taylor gleefully told one of his favourite stories, about how quickly the best man could shovel a pile of coal. 'You have told us the effect on the pile,' an exasperated committee member replied, but 'what about the effect on the man?'

The effect on the man was always exhaustion. In 1911, moulders at an arsenal in Watertown, Massachusetts, refused to work under the eye of a timekeeper. Pouring a mould and making a gun carriage usually took fifty-three minutes but Taylor's timekeeper told the moulders it could be done in twenty-four. The men struck and during the investigation that followed it emerged that Taylor had told his timekeeper that the stopwatch was really a prop and that it was better to make 'a rough guess'.

'Speedy' Taylor, as he was disparagingly known, did not last long in any steel mill he ever entered. In the early 1900s, there were strikes at McKees Rock, East Hammond, Lawrence, Passaic, Akron, Detroit, and Paterson, all factories that had adopted his methods. In Paterson, silk workers went on strike after weavers were suddenly expected to work twice as many looms as before. Workers who did not conform to the new standards were fired. So was Taylor two years later and he left behind him a company with terrible industrial relations. He also took with him the $100,000 dollars he had charged in fees (the equivalent of $2.5 million today).

The governing ideas of Taylorism were that management is a skill and that this skill has the properties of a science. Yet when he testified to Congress, Taylor admitted that the adjustments he made to his calculations, to work out how much a man could do in a day, varied from 20 per cent to 225 per cent. The claim that management is scientific ought to have eliminated guesswork of this kind. Taylor never published the data on which his pig iron or other conclusions were based. His method, in the end, was a series of exhortations to work harder, timed by a stopwatch.

Extravagant claims have since been advanced on Taylor's behalf. In *The Rise of the Knowledge Society*, Peter Drucker offered the rather silly judgement that Taylor's *The Principles of Scientific Management* was 'the most powerful as well as the most lasting contribution America has made to Western thought since the Federalist papers'. Drucker went on to say that, though Darwin, Marx and Freud were usually held to be the intellectual founding fathers of the modern world, 'Marx would be taken out and replaced by Taylor if there were any justice'.

At the same time as the ideas of scientific management were changing the way people thought about their own work, a parallel shift was taking place in the conduct of business. The pioneer of the change was Henry Ford. Ford was a complex man who somehow combined the democratic desire to create good cars that his workers could afford with a virulent anti-Semitism and an inflated sense of importance which meant he contemplated running for President on a more or less fascist prospectus in 1924.

Ford's legacy, though, is in his business methods rather than his frivolous politics. The production of the Model-T in 1908 changed the world because it brought mobility to the masses. Fordism, a term coined by Antonio Gramsci in the *Prison Notebooks*, was characterized by three principles which have a clear resemblance to Taylor's claims to scientific management:

1. A standardized process in which nothing is made by hand; instead all products emerge from moulds and mechanized procedures tended by unskilled workers.
2. The use of assembly lines fitted out with special-purpose tools.

3. A high basic wage for workers which enables them to afford the products that roll off the assembly line.

Taylor and Ford were both notorious in their time. Taylor inspired Yevgeny Zamyatin to write *We*, the dystopia which George Orwell read as he wrote *Nineteen Eighty-Four*. Aldous Huxley dated the years AF (Anno Ford, in the year of our Ford) in *Brave New World*. The expression My Ford is used as an imprecation instead of My Lord and the crucifix is replaced with a Ford Model-T.

The abiding bequest of Taylorism and Fordism was a shift in perception. Business was no longer thought to be a branch of the humanities. Measured, timed, broken into its parts and re-assembled by machine, the mission that Taylor and Ford were intent upon was that business should migrate to the province of the sciences.

Mechanization has greatly enhanced productivity and there are, of course, better and worse ways to run a factory but none of that makes business a science like Physics or Chemistry. Yet that quest, initiated by Taylor and Ford, is exactly what then started in the academy. The first business school to open its doors had been in Paris in 1819 but the first in the United States, which presaged an era of immense growth, was the Wharton School at the University of Pennsylvania in 1881.

The Tuck School of Business at Dartmouth College followed in 1900 as the first graduate school. Tuck conferred the first advanced degree in business, a Master of Science in Commercial Sciences.

In 1908, Edwin Gay, a Harvard Economics professor, who had been consistently frustrated in his attempts to open a business school, visited Taylor in Philadelphia. He came away convinced that the scientific method could apply to business and that this would make the idea of a business school easier to sell to the Harvard authorities. Harvard Business School opened that year to offer its MBA programme. Gay was its first dean and Taylor delivered a series of lectures in Cambridge, Massachusetts, every year until his death. The number of MBA students at Harvard increased quickly, from 80 in 1908, to over 300 in 1920. By 1930 there were over a thousand.

This move into the academy is an echo of the argument prosecuted long before, in the fifth century BC, by the sophists. Taylor's principles were a temptation to think that business acumen was a classifiable and teachable skill. Management, which had before Taylor been a process of intuition, moved into the classroom. Business, once a practical skill, began to acquire a theoretical bent and started to assert itself as a subject in its own right. This establishing of business as a field of study was accompanied by the emergence of the term 'Economics' in the last years of the nineteenth century. Until then, scholars with an interest in commercial activity had studied a broad subject called Political Economy which was the study of production and trade and their relationship with laws, custom and government. Sir James Steuart's *An Inquiry into the Principles of Political Economy* of 1761 was the first book to name the discipline in its title.

Political Economy was a discipline with a wide sweep which derived from eighteenth-century moral philosophy. The world's first professorship in Political Economy had been established in 1754 at the University of Naples Federico II. In 1805, Thomas Malthus had become England's first professor of Political Economy, at the East India Company College. The flowering of the tradition came with the work of Adam Smith and David Ricardo. The topic of Smith's and Ricardo's great works was that economic relations of men always had a political and a moral dimension. Smith's *The Wealth of Nations* is a founding text of economics but a book that is rich in philosophical and historical inquiry.

The term 'economics' was first proposed in William Jevons's *A General Mathematical Theory of Political Economy*, published in 1862. Jevons hoped that 'economics' would become 'the recognized name of a science'. But the book which accelerated the movement of economics towards mathematics – and towards the illusion of scientific certainty – was Alfred Marshall's *Principles of Economics* published first in 1890 and many times thereafter. This is the landmark moment, the point at which Political Economy as a distinct academic field was replaced in universities by the separate discipline of Economics.

By 1920, Political Economy had largely disappeared and Economics had become the preferred term for the subject. The field of study narrowed as the political and social context shrank. Cut adrift from the study of the economy, Politics also floated free, to the detriment of understanding in both disciplines. Political Economy had been devoted to the essential truths that politics is always economic, economics is always political and both are always moral. That linkage was lost as Economics began to assert its credentials as a branch of mathematics or a discipline that stands in a line of ancestry from Physics.

Where Political Economy had been rooted in Moral Philosophy, the new discipline of Economics sought objective knowledge free from prior values. Marshall wanted Economics to resemble Newtonian physics, to be formal, precise and elegant. The divorce initiated by Marshall was confirmed by the publication, in 1947, of Paul Samuelson's *Foundations of Economic Analysis*. Samuelson called mathematics 'the natural language of economics' and it is easy to see the attraction.

Politics was the domain of ideology and contested argument. Mathematics substituted for its rhetorical dispute the pleasure of certainty and precision. With Samuelson the connection between economics and politics was severed and what he insisted was a gain is, in truth, a severe loss. As Kenneth Boulding put it: 'Mathematics brought rigor to Economics. Unfortunately it also brought mortis.'

The claims that production ought to be mechanical, that management is a science and that business is a separate field of study, are all landmarks. Together, they help to create the conditions in which a new, historically ill-informed and damaging idea of the company emerged. Business, which was for Seebohm Rowntree, intrinsic to the conduct of social life, started to become detached from the everyday. It became esoteric and specialist and disclosed its secrets only to the native speakers of a secret language. This foolish and damaging change took place in defiance of the history of the company. The joint stock company is, in point of fact, the creation of public law, specifically Robert Lowe's Joint Stock Companies Act of 1862. The Act introduced the idea of limited liability and created the enterprise of the public limited company. The Act, almost forgotten now, was so heralded in its day that Gilbert and Sullivan wrote a comic opera in celebration called *Dystopia, Limited*.

The import of the Act was that it linked the joint stock company to the public realm from the very act of its creation. They were, from inception, *public* limited companies rather than purely private organizations. To write and speak in terms that are inaccessible to the general public implies that the company operates in an enchanted realm to which the ordinary person is denied access. When the language of business travels too far from the common popular idiom, the company grows apart from its host society. In an era in which the best companies are trying to rediscover obligations beyond the narrow domain of their shareholders, it makes no sense to speak a native tongue that says the opposite. To speak plainly and clearly is therefore a business imperative.

The abandonment of ordinary language is damaging and dangerous. Where the language of business avoids ordinary discourse, crimes and misdemeanours are easier. Jargon can make wrongdoing sound innocuous. In 2008, the complex mathematics of highly geared financial packages exceeded the capacity both of regulators to set appropriate guidelines and of most practitioners to understand the risks. If the language of sub-prime had not been so clogged with technical jargon, the world might have been alerted to the fact that a disaster was about to unfold.

Friedrich Nietzsche saw all this coming in *On Truth and Lies in a Non-Moral Sense*, published in 1873 in which he wrote of the 'mobile army of metaphors ... which are worn out and without sensuous power; coins which have lost their pictures and now matter only as metal, no longer as coins'. Every generation in business invents its own mobile army. You can speak the leveraged, value-added idiom of financial services. You can talk bandwidth off-line with the tech bores. You can talk battles and frontlines with the disruptors. Or you can embrace the organic evolution and self-actualizing of the new age.

The detachment of business from the society in which it is hosted has acquired its own vocabulary, in both the theory and practice of business, which brings us back to Seebohm Rowntree and Satya Nadella. Mr Rowntree's language is that of a man whose company is part of the nation in which it works. Mr Nadella is talking high-priest voodoo. Mr Rowntree shares a language with his audience. Mr Nadella talks to them *de haut en bas*.

All of these new vocabularies take ostentatious relish in how little they sound like ordinary life. Their mobile army of metaphors are dead on arrival. They fail the test of clarity. Business executives are damaging their own character with every utterance and yet there is surprisingly little tuition on offer. Remarkably, for a subject in which the skill of persuasion is paramount, the business school curricula offer no serious guidance on how to communicate. They disseminate a private language but they do not see fit to analyse it. The language of business is simply taken for granted as the appropriate way to speak. In the absence of any help from that quarter, the dictionary of usage that follows will have to stand instead.

The Means of Persuasion

But before we come to the individual items, the horrors of poor usage and the comic creations of business-speak, it would be good to establish some principles for usage. Three enemies of good writing stalk the pages of business brochures and haunt the halls in which executives stand to speak: orthodoxy, abstraction and jargon.

It is an axiom of modern business writing that anyone claiming to be unique is in the grip of the latest orthodoxy. Read any number of mission statements (in fact, one is enough) and you soon notice the same well-worn turns of phrase in each one. Every claim to unrivalled uniqueness reads exactly like every other claim to unrivalled uniqueness. Bereft of character or distinguishing features, mission statements seem to be assembled from readily available parts, like the sections, as Orwell memorably put it, of a prefabricated hen house.

After its unerring sameness, the next most notable characteristic of much business writing is its windy abstraction. So much of it reads like a conspiracy against meaning. Writers stampede towards the vague and the abstract and away from the precise and the concrete. Frightened to commit to any hard statement, their writing floats up into inflated euphemism which is never quite false but never quite true either. There is a strong sense of nothing quite being said, at great length.

The interminable feeling is exacerbated by strange word choice. Jargon, which originally referred to the inarticulate twittering and chattering of birds, goes back at least as far as Chaucer. In *The Merchant's Tale*, Chaucer gives us an extended description of the wedding night of a particularly prolific knight called January, and his bride May. The fun goes on all night and then, as day is breaking, January sits up in bed and says 'and full of jargon as a flekked pye [magpie]', which just means that he goes on a lot, not making all that much sense.

That much of Chaucer's lost meaning has remained because this truly is the golden age of meaningless jargon. The attraction of jargon in business is its capacity to make us feel exalted. Needlessly complex language is a counterfeit signal of expertise. Jargon conveniently seems to erase conflict because when nothing is being said there can be no disagreement. Jargon elevates routine processes and invests them with the fake glamour of obscurity.

Genuine fields of scholarship, such as epidemiology or inorganic chemistry, have technical vocabularies for which there are no colloquial alternatives. Jargon, by contrast, is the deliberate translation of ordinary ideas into complicated word patterns in order to exclude the uninitiated. Business associates mimic their seniors to show that they belong. It makes a low art form sound like the highest science. But business is not a science. A business involves a complex array of human interactions. It is part history, part sociology and part anthropology. It is a realm not of scientific proof but of rhetorical proof.

The deficiencies of orthodoxy, abstraction and jargon define what good writing lacks, but can we specify what good writing should include? There is something inexorable about the best prose, like the flow of water in a river. It is as if every word could only have been the one chosen and not some other word. Though the sophists were right to insist that writing can be taught – you can, of course, get better – good style is not to be found, readily packaged, in style guides. There is an abundance of style guides available (they are listed in the Bibliography) and many of the authors are distinguished – George Orwell, Kingsley Amis, Stephen King, P. D. James and Stephen Pinker, for example. The best of them offers serviceable guidelines and ways of avoiding infelicities. But a good prose piece is no more the sum of style guide entries than a fine meal is simply a case of reading the recipe properly.

Where the style guides become fastidious and fussy they will be actively harmful to your prose. There can be no fixed rules because a living language changes in the mouths of its speakers. Everyone who speaks a language is simultaneously writing its dictionary. To borrow Stephen Pinker's description, when it comes to language the lunatics are in charge of the asylum. This is therefore not a book in which you will be harangued about punctuation or subjected to stern lectures on correct grammar. There will be no pompous judgements on whether it is right to say you and I rather than you and me or any insistence on the precise meaning of the word decimate.

The aim is at once simpler and more important. The aim is to write clearly and so what follows is a series of suggestions, with reasons attached, rather than commandments. You will not encounter rules in this book but you will encounter choices. The aim is to choose well and to thereby achieve the aim of saying precisely what you mean to say.

Though the style guides are usually too prescriptive and too full of personal eccentricities passed off as rules, they do, taken as a whole, provide some reliable principles for good writing. There are three aids to clarity which it is as well to keep in mind while writing: simplicity, precision and brevity. Treat these three as guardians of your prose style to ward off the enemy forces of complexity, vagueness and long-windedness.

Simplicity is a virtue that can be difficult to honour. It is possible to be simple when, but only when, the speaker has a central case to make. Where the speaker has no topic there will be no clarity and the argument will spiral out into complexity. There is no better way to be boring, as Voltaire once said, than to leave nothing out.

The failsafe way of staying simple is to avoid at work any phrase you would be reluctant to use at home. As Hippocrates said: 'The chief virtue that language can have is clearness and nothing detracts from it so much as the use of unfamiliar words.' The best advice is to address your remarks to an educated lay person who does not inhabit your world. That will ensure you dramatically simplify, and therefore clarify, your language. This is certainly the advice from the ancient authorities. In the *Poetics*, Aristotle cautioned against 'strange words' and 'anything that deviates from ordinary modes of speech'. In *On Invention*, Cicero wrote that writing should be clear, plausible and brief and should seek to emulate 'the practice of ordinary people'. Cicero returned to this idea in his later work *De Oratore*, where he states that 'the greatest vice is to disdain conventional language and ordinary feelings'.

Hazlitt put the same point well: 'To write a genuine, familiar or truly English style is to write as anyone would speak in common conversation . . .'

In the most effective part of his essay *Politics and the English Language*, George Orwell lampoons five terrible passages of writing and notes that the feature they share is a lack of precision. A mark of poor writing is that it is impossible to edit. Precise writing can be summarized by referring to the concrete details and simply taking out the connecting tissue. Poor writing has nothing but tissue but there is nothing to connect because no precise points are being made. Language that is simple and precise will make a straightforward point quickly.

Which raises the third virtue. Good writing should be exactly as long as it needs to be and no longer. 'When you wish to instruct, be brief,' wrote Cicero. 'Every word that is unnecessary only pours over the side of a brimming mind.' To be simple, precise and yet brief will take some prior thought. Pascal's famous line comes to mind: I'm sorry to have written you such a long letter. I would have written a shorter one but I didn't have the time. In a memorandum dated 9 August 1940, Winston Churchill asked his staff to strip from their submissions any material not germane to the main point: 'To do our work,' he wrote, 'we all have to read a mass of papers. Nearly all of them are far too long. This wastes time, while energy has to be spent in looking for the essential points.' Churchill then made the link between the expression of an idea and the thought that preceded it. 'The discipline of setting out the real points concisely will prove an aid to clearer thinking,' he wrote.

Simplicity, precision and brevity is the trinity of virtues that will help a writer to be clear and clarity is the pre-condition of being persuasive. It is not, however, a guarantee. Not every clear statement is automatically persuasive. Indeed, the very clarity of a statement, with all obfuscation stripped back, can reveal just how unpersuasively stark some propositions can be. The skilful writer needs to turn a clear argument to persuasive effect and that requires an understanding of what the ancient writers described as the rhetorical appeals. *In The Art of Rhetoric*, Aristotle defines three manners of persuasive appeal: ethos, pathos and logos which we can translate as character, emotion and argument. A balance needs to be struck between the three different appeals and in most business writing the weights of the three rhetorical appeals are all wrong. When modern business writing is not buzzing with words it is being dried out by numerical proofs. There is too much rationality and too little colour.

Character, which Aristotle described as 'the basis of persuasion' and 'the most effective type of proof', is the bedrock of good writing. A voice gives the words the stamp of an individual. The ethos of our voice is the way we create trust. This is a virtue we call character in a person and brand in a business. As Isocrates, an influential teacher and writer on rhetoric from the fourth century BC reflected in his autobiography, *Antidosis*, 'the argument which is made by a man's life is of more weight than that which is furnished by words'.

The same point is made, with characteristic subtlety, by Jane Austen in her novel *Persuasion*. The appeal of ethos is routinely invoked as a source of authority in a society so conscious of origins. The patriarch Sir Walter Elliot is reluctant to let the large family home he can no longer afford to run but his objections fall when an Admiral, rather than a mere Mr as he puts it, applies to take on the tenancy. Later, Captain Wentworth, the male lead who is destined to marry the novel's heroine, Anne Elliot, is described as 'a young man who had nothing but himself to recommend him'. He had ethos and, though Anne is too wilful for it to clinch the issue, it helps.

The behavioural scientists have provided a body of experimental evidence to support what Aristotle understood by observation. We make rapid character assessments which we use as prisms through which we judge what is said. In *Messengers: Who We Listen To, Who We Don't, and Why*, Marks and Martin show how these instinctive decisions are made in quick-fire character assessments. We respond to a series of attributes that hit our senses long before a rational word has been uttered. Our initial perceptions of competence, dominance, attractiveness, warmth, vulnerability and charisma combine to draw a character sketch. Our brains take all of a tenth of a second to register whether we regard a given person as trustworthy. Marks and Martin, and all those who have made the same point, are simply providing statistical proof for an ancient insight. They are Aristotle and Isocrates with graphs.

The task of communication therefore is to take command of that immediate impression made by character. A character is, after all, is not just something we are said to have, the set of properties and habits that make us who we are. It is also something that we play and the character we present to the world is always an amalgam of the traits we have in our repertoire arranged for each setting. The idea of character is, at bottom, rhetorical.

The trust that derives from character has three sources: expertise, moral virtue and likeability. Credentials lend a rightful authority to a speaker. It says a great deal about a witness if, during a pandemic, she is introduced as a Professor of Epidemiology. Moral virtue is seen to best effect when a speaker is thought to be disinterested. It is easier to seem pure in motive if you have no stake in the outcome. When you do, which in the world of business is most of the time, the morally virtuous strategy is to be transparent. A reputation for plain dealing then helps cultivate the virtue of likeability which Aristotle defines as 'the goodwill between a speaker and the audience'.

When a recognizable character takes the stage a healthy fraction of the act of persuasion takes place at once and continues invisibly throughout. That character then needs to be supplied with an emotional life. What Aristotle calls pathos is the claim that it is 'through emotion that an audience is led to persuasion'. Quintilian writes that 'a speech will not have sufficient impact nor will it be fully authoritative if it can only affect the ears . . . rather than as they are presented or displayed to the eyes of the mind.' Pathos is the art of making someone feel the force of what you say. In the battle between reasons and the passions, reason is the slave and passion the master.

In *Persuasion*, Anne Elliot, who is a reflective and thoughtful woman, nevertheless writes off the matrimonial appeal of her cousin by noting that 'Mr Elliot was rational, discreet, polished, – but he was not open. There was never any burst of feeling, any warmth of indignation or delight, at the evil or good of others.' In a word, he was not persuasive.

This philosophical and literary insight can now be supplemented by a body of research. Jennifer S. Lerner and her colleagues at Harvard University produced, in 2014, a paper called *Emotion and Decision Making* which is a comprehensive gathering of the evidence about how human beings balance emotion and reason. It shows that when the emotional connection is severed, human beings struggle to come to any decision at all. In a world in which we are saturated in information, an emotional response is a valuable short-cut, a heuristic that encodes important knowledge that is easy and quick to digest.

We have already travelled a long way from standard business language and this distance can make executives feel uncomfortable. The need to impart emotion into business communication is often misunderstood. To bring emotion into business communication does not mean a compunction to tug at the heartstrings with distressing autobiographical stories. We are not writing about the death of Little Nell. To be emotional, in a business context, means two simple things. It is a demand to write or speak in pictures and an imperative to include stories which feature real people.

Much of what needs to be said in business is intrinsically rather dry. Yet it does not take much effort, in most instances, to include some emotional content. The best medium for transmitting an emotional message is visual. Human memory is fallible but it improves significantly when we are asked to recall images rather than prose arguments. The visual memory is encoded in the medial temporal lobe of the brain, which is the same place in which the emotions are processed. Visual information transmitted to the brain is processed many thousands of times faster than text. What we see or touch lingers longer in the memory than what we merely hear. The task of good writing is to make the reader see something in their mind's eye. The practised writer can summarize a complex argument in a single visual image.

The process of retrieval from the memory is helped if the image in question contains or refers to a person. The human propensity to tell stories is how we make sense of the world. Business writing is usually heavy with statistical proof but those points will tell no story unless they are embodied in a narrative proof. Which is a different level of truth than arithmetic. Narrative proof tells moral and philosophical truths.

The meeting point between the ancient rhetoricians and the contemporary behavioural psychologists has been found again. People hearing a tense moment in a story experience a spike in their cortisol levels and when they empathize with a character, their oxytocin levels rise. There may be hard-wired evolutionary reasons for this, perhaps because stories bind us together or because they contain important survival information. Whatever the primeval roots of the behaviour, we know that facts embedded like jewellery in the setting of a story are more persuasive than facts left to stand alone.

At the centre of all stories is a person, or people, on whom the causes act and who act as causes in their turn. Imagine the story of *Oliver Twist* in which the eponymous hero was not named and Fagin, Bill Sikes, Nancy and the Artful Dodger were all deleted. Imagine that, instead of the parade of characters designed to illustrate, collectively, the moral that good can survive many depredations in the world, Dickens had written a corporate monograph in which he had referred to the way that good plans can be derailed by evil forces for a time though the company can still prevail if everyone sticks at it. The story, shorn of characters and thereby of character, would be bloodless and lifeless. Everything memorable about the story is an incident that happens to a character – Oliver demanding more food, Nancy taking Oliver to refuge by night, Nancy's murder by Bill Sikes. Even the authorial commentary by Dickens, as vivid as it is, does not stay in the memory. The emotional heart of the book, and therefore its persuasive message, is contained in the connection forged by the dramas of stylized people. With obvious alteration of details and intent, this is something that good writing in all contexts needs to emulate.

Good writing needs character and it needs an emotional connection but it will fall apart without discipline. The third of Aristotle's rhetorical appeals is logos which is the rational case that is being made. If pathos is the attempt to make the listener feel the same as you, logos is the attempt to make the listener think the same.

The importance of logos will not be lost on most corporate writers who tend to be rational to a fault. It is though, for all their dry excess, imperative to assemble relevant evidence and illustrations, organized into a chain of argument. Claims need to be enumerated, ordered and supported. They need to proceed logically from one assertion to the next, which builds and deepens the insight. All of this needs to be bound around a tight structure which is the framework on which an argument hangs.

Writing that is simple, precise and brief, full of character, emotion and sound logic is not the alpha and omega of great style. These are the necessary parts but they offer no guarantee of elegance. Writing that obeys these dictates can still be pedestrian but it cannot avoid being clear and that is sufficient ambition for the moment. The task is to be clear and, by being clear, to be persuasive, not to write prose to rival the last few pages of *The Great Gatsby*. Indeed, anyone capable even of writing to the standard of F. Scott Fitzgerald is probably wasted in the corporate communications department in any case.

Those three appeals – character, emotion and argument – are not virtues for different occasions. Persuasive communication will, in all contexts, contain all three. The balance may differ according to time, place and purpose but it is rare that a characterless text will persuade on the sole basis of its ineluctable rationality or that an emotional address will succeed if it lacks any sense of order. The question is not which appeal to choose but how to find the right balance.

There can be no definitive answer to this question and no formula to work it out, but it is safe to say that, in the corporate world in the developed economies, the balance is awry. Every company should conduct an audit of the balance of its appeals across all the formats in which it seeks to persuade. The overwhelming majority of such audits would find that the communication was so heavily weighted towards the rational that any sense of character or gesture towards emotion was invisible.

This is by a long way not the optimally most persuasive balance. The majority of words that are featured in the glossary of strange usage that follows in Part Two (*The Dictionary of Good and Bad Choices*) are attempts to create an ersatz scientific vocabulary for the human enterprise of business. All the changes in the language serve to strip out character and emotion in favour of an apparent rationality. The effect is neither persuasive nor even especially rational. Choked in words that aspire to meaning and fall short, so much business communication persuades nobody of anything except the determination to stop reading.

Aristotle thought that character and emotion mattered a good deal more than the argument itself but then Aristotle never had the pleasure of preparing the quarterly earnings statement. A good rational case needs to be made but this case will be heard and will be more persuasive, if it is embellished by an emotional case and embedded in a resolute character. If the rational content were merely halved, it would be a revolution in the way people in business spoke, and all for the better. It would be, in fact, a return to the way people in business spoke once upon a time, in the distant days when they spoke very much like the rest of us.

To Be Clear

Which was, if you recall, how Seebohm Rowntree sounded in *The Human Factor in Business*:

> That is why I have written this book, which largely consists of a description of the way in which the directors of the Cocoa Works, York, have tried to solve some of the human problems of business administration. I deal with the subject under five heads – Wages, Hours, Economic Security of the Workers, Working Conditions,

Joint Control, – and in each section I indicate the end
we have in view, the means by which we try to achieve it,
and the extent of our success. I should be the last to claim
any special merit for our methods, but we have received
so much help from others, that it seemed incumbent on
us to throw our experience into the common stock of
knowledge, in the hope that we may thus repay, in some
measure, the debt we owe to the experience of other firms.

Now that we have been steeped in contemporary language,
we can correct Mr Rowntree's clarity. Here is how an articulate
and native speaker of business might render this passage today:

I have written this book for the purposes of describing the
best-in-class way the global Cocoa Works management
team have done a deep dive into the key challenges of
the business administration piece. I architect the subject under five heads – Compensation, Customer-centric
Behaviours, Authentic Working, the Associate Experience, Innovative Partnerships – and in each section I
state our objectives, our deliverables and the execution
algorithms and metrics on a balanced scorecard. We can
catalyse our own execution and we are taking on board
the many learnings from the ideations of others. In the

B2B space we have aligned our experience, mission and optionality so that, going forward, we are on the same page as we drive the business strategy forward.

There is no need to write and speak like this. Opaque language of this sort is both the consequence of poor thinking and the cause of more poor thinking. The more that corporate language retreats into its own redoubt the less of a connection it retains with the listening public. This is bad for commerce and bad for the reputation of business, which amounts to the same thing. If business language is going to return to earth the senior executives need to lead the way. In 1943, Robert Wood Johnson, a founding family member of Johnson & Johnson, wrote the following mission statement for the company which is a model of good corporate writing because it is plain and does not try to complicate simple things or hide what the business does in flowery diction.

We believe our first responsibility is to the patients, doctors and nurses, to mothers and fathers and all others who use our products and services. In meeting their needs everything we do must be of high quality. We must constantly strive to provide value, reduce our costs and maintain reasonable prices. Customers' orders must

be serviced promptly and accurately. Our business partners must have an opportunity to make a fair profit.
We are responsible to our employees who work with us
throughout the world. We must provide an inclusive work
environment where each person must be considered as
an individual. We must respect their diversity and dignity
and recognize their merit ...

Business executives need to talk and write like this. They
need to stop talking in code and have the courage to be plain,
in the knowledge that they have something to say and it would
be better for the world to understand what it was. It is possible to banish all management-speak but the impulse has to
come from the top. If within the firm advancement seems to
depend on speaking an alien language, ambitious people will
learn the lingo. But the way that language trickles down a
company is also cause for optimism. If the chief executive of
every Fortune 50 and every FTSE-100 company made a vow
to forswear business nonsense, it would soon wither.

The task of being clear in written prose has never mattered
more. General popular illiteracy was eliminated from European societies in the latter half of the nineteenth century but,
up to the invention of the internet, most people did not have
a great deal of cause to write. Now that more than half the

47

world has access to email, social media and instant messaging, we are writing more than we ever have. In a single day we type out 500 million tweets, 65 billion WhatsApp messages, and 294 billion emails. The World Economic Forum has estimated that 90 per cent of the world's data has been produced in the last two years alone. Most of this written work is for private use but plenty of it is business communication. More commerce is conducted in written form than ever before. It has never been more necessary to write persuasively.

As well as offering advice on composition, this book has proposed a rhetorical method of thinking which will help to avoid some of the egregious examples that are littered through the dictionary. Business is an act of persuasion and so strategic thought would benefit from a rhetorical process of careful deliberation, forensic testing and vivid display. Writing which is simple, precise and brief will meet the aim of being clear and will avoid the tempting errors of orthodoxy, abstraction and jargon. Close attention to the balance of rhetorical appeals will infuse business writing with enough character and emotion to leaven the rational argument. This will be an appropriate balance for an activity which is part of the human enterprises and not a member of the natural sciences.

The prize is considerable and not just for hard-pressed readers. With clearer persuasion, business will come back from the journey towards specialization which is, if it extends too far, a journey towards oblivion. Businesses will resume their place at the centre of a liberal democratic capitalist society because they are once more operating within the centre of its language. The esteem and renown of business will rise as its distinguished representatives once again use all the available means of persuasion for the benefit, and perhaps even sometimes the delight, of the audience which now listens attentively to what they have to say.

The language that is used in public can be clear and we will understand one another better if it is. There is no good reason to write and speak badly when it is possible, indeed it is easier, to write and speak well. Every business executive has it within their gift to realize the ambition of this book which is simply this: to be clear.

PART TWO

The Dictionary of Good

and Bad Choices

A

Abstraction and abstract nouns. It is a good principle, wherever possible, to be as detailed and concrete as you can. A retreat into *abstract nouns* gives a sense of elevation always lifting you away from precise meaning. When the abstract nouns start to pile up it makes your writing generic. Too much abstraction is usually a sign that the writer has a space to fill but nothing to say. Try to translate every abstract noun into a concrete detail. If no translation can be done, the text is empty. Look how unconvincingly distant this text, from the Microsoft annual report, sounds: 'We fundamentally believe that we need a culture founded in a growth mindset. We also need to actively seek diversity and embrace inclusion to create a culture where everyone can do their best work.'[1] Why 'embrace inclusion' rather than include someone and why not illustrate the idea, not with this deadening prose but with a picture of a person who is telling their story?

In *The Sense of Style*, Stephen Pinker supplies a useful list of generic words that have the effect of distancing the reader from the intended meaning. If you find yourself using some of the words Pinker lists, like *level*, *strategy*, *issues*, *perspective*, *prospect*, *model*, *approach*, *assumption*, *concept*, *condition*, *content*, *framework*, *process*, *range* or *tendency*, ask yourself whether you could not have written something more precise. As Pinker asks: 'could you recognize a "level" or a "perspective" if you met one in the street?'

Acronyms. The best practice is to write out the full name on first usage with the *acronym* in brackets and then use the acronym thereafter. The same applies with abbreviations. Hence London Stock Exchange (LSE) and LSE on each subsequent usage. Try to be sparing, though. A text clogged with acronyms can be hard to follow, especially if the acronyms are unfamiliar.

Action. When you use this word as a verb (to *action*), you simply mean you are going to do something. Or you intend to reply or write or answer, or some other specific action. You will write better if you say what it is you intend to do rather than placing everything under the generic cover of 'actions' or, even worse, 'actionables'. The same strictures can be entered about the verb 'to deliver' and the things subsequently delivered, the 'deliverables'. You ought to wince every time you say it so that 'deliverables' becomes literally undeliverable.

Active verbs. Some style guides become peremptory at this point and demand that you always use *active verbs* and avoid the passive voice altogether. Even Orwell is tempted to say so. There is, however, no such rule. Indeed, Orwell illustrates the point by accident. In *Politics and the English Language*, the essay in which he deplores the use of the passive voice, Orwell actually uses it himself and thereby proves himself wrong: 'The passive voice is wherever possible used in preference to the active.' The passive voice is perfectly acceptable if a sense of being passive is what you want to communicate.

Most of the time, in business, it isn't, though, and so the passive voice is usually inappropriate rather than wrong. You will generally want to convey a mood of action and enterprise. The passive voice often distances you from the action and attributes causation to an impersonal force. In a lot of business writing it is used as a distancing device, because the principal is too scared to associate him or herself with the direct action in case it all goes wrong. It sounds feeble to say, for example, that a decision has been made to close your bank account. We learn nothing, probably deliberately, about who made that decision and why.

Try to make sure that there is always someone in your writing who is acting. If there is an implied person and that implied person is doing something, your writing will avoid descending into passive dullness. Try to be bolder. Try to have more courage. Try to be more direct. Otherwise, you end up sounding like you are not running your own business but that it all happens mysteriously by the dullest alchemy imaginable, as in this 2020 BAT strategy document: 'Our business will be further enabled by simplifying our management structure, truly embracing digital transformation, rigorously managing our cost base, and enhancing our internal culture.'[2]

Actualize. A verb that it would be better not to *actualize*. Nothing should ever really be actualized, not even yourself. In most contexts it will mean 'make real' or even 'make'. Or it is used to add a veneer of interest to the dull fact that something just happened. This is not a new business coinage. Actualize first appeared in Samuel Taylor Coleridge's periodical *The Friend* in 1809: 'To make our Feelings, with their vital warmth, actualize our Reason'. It is a rare event, though, that a sentence can be written containing the word actualize that isn't ugly, as this usage by John Hert, CEO of Arcoro illustrates: 'I am incredibly excited to join the Arcoro family and to help lead the company to actualize its extensive potential to serve more customers through organic growth and strategic acquisitions.'[3]

Adverbs. Before using an adverb to qualify a verb try to think of a more precise verb instead. For example, better to say 'he accelerated' than 'he went more quickly'. Adverbs are also rarely a good way of beginning a sentence. There is no need to start a sentence by telling the reader 'Ironically ...' If your point does contain any irony, we will find out soon enough and then we will feel patronized by your instruction to look for it. Irony probably isn't a common technique in business, in any case.

Aggregate. Better as a noun (the aggregate of a set) rather than a verb (we aggregated the items), not because it doesn't make sense but because it is imprecise. Even an innocuous word like *aggregate* conceals details. You may have added the items up. Or you may have brought them together. Two different processes and you could tell us which one you used, rather than aggregate all the various processes under the generic term 'aggregate'. When Amazon tells us, in its 2019 annual report, that the 'World Health Organization is leveraging our cloud to build large-scale data lakes [and] aggregate epidemiological country data',[4] it is not clear what is actually being said (and not just because it is hard to imagine how, or indeed whether, one might leverage a cloud and how that leveraging might result in a lake full of data). They probably mean that they have gathered and are publishing data from lots of countries but the slipshod use of the more complex-sounding 'aggregate' has obscured the meaning. 'Aggregate', which derives from the Latin *aggreg* , which has the same root as *gregarious* and which means to flock together, is best used to denote the melding of different sets of data.

A-ha. Not, in this context, a Norwegian band who had a number 2 hit with 'Take On Me' in October 1985. Instead, *a-ha* is a corporate buzzword for the moment you realize something, replacing the old, and slightly less cringe-worthy corporate buzzword, the light-bulb moment. 'For prospects and clients who can potentially have the biggest business impact for us, we help onboard the whole team to help quickly bring them closer to their "aha" moment', as someone wrote in a NetHunt CRM document.[5] Surely you feel daft saying this. I hope you will now. Knowing me, knowing you. A-ha!

Alignment. 'To ensure alignment with shareholder interests, a significant proportion of the potential remuneration of the executive directors is variable and is therefore performance related.' This comes from the Barclays strategic report 2018[6] but there are legions of examples. *Alignment* is a word that is much in vogue but usually means less than its dictionary definition. Do you mean that you have informed everyone? That you popped by the sales department and let them know? Did you send an 'All Users' email? Or do you mean that they agreed with you? Did they say so? Did they mean it, if they did? Alignment is often used as an unconvincing synonym for agreement but it doesn't quite mean the same as agreement. In all likelihood, the apparently aligned colleagues won't quite agree. When the word 'alignment' comes to mind, try to say what you mean instead.

American English. The language written and spoken in America differs in some well-known respects from its usage in England. Much business writing has to work in both places so some conventions on usage and spelling need to be established. The first thought is to avoid the snobbish and unhistorical idea that the English have rightful ownership of a language which the Americans insist upon subverting. This is nonsense. The most partisan advocate of the alternative, that American English teems with the life lost in the flat English variety, is H. L. Mencken whose 1919 book *The American Language: An Inquiry into the Development of English in the United States* was an extended plea for the linguistic ingenuity of the Americans.

Mencken is making the essential point that languages change, and that usage can be evocative and interesting when it departs from accepted convention.

The wonder is, in fact, that so powerful a nation as America has not had more influence on English than it has. The linguist Max Weinreich once said that a language is a dialect with an army and a navy. The best policy therefore is not to worry too much about what is correct and adopt a clear corporate position on vocabulary and spelling. If you want to see *the color of your money* in New York but try a different *colour* in London, then there is nothing wrong with that. Many words which we might now regard as quintessentially American – *gotten* as the past participle of *get* or *fall* for *autumn* – originated in England, were adopted in America and subsequently disappeared in the mother country. Besides, *fall* is a lovely visual evocation of the season, a much better word than autumn. *Fall* remained in use in England until the second half of the nineteenth century and why it fell out of favour then is a mystery. Plenty of spellings that we now regard as correct – such as *magick* contracted to *magic* – came from American usage. Which of these serviceable English words – *blizzard*, *talented*, *reliable* – would you like to do without? They were all imports from America once. Do you never say the words *commuter*, *telephone*, *radio* or *currency* which are all of American origin? Two countries that trade so freely will always trade words and it is to the benefit of both that they do. Britain has been an open nation, historically and that suits language formation just fine, to adopt a good colloquial American expression.

Architect. Daniel Liebeskind is an *architect.* When he is at work he thinks, draws, designs. He does not architect. That is not to say that the word does not exist. Any word that gets used exists, by definition. Indeed, the *Oxford English Dictionary* provides citations to this effect as far back as 1813. Keats wrote in a letter that 'this was architected thus by the great Oceanus'. Yet here the sense is figurative and transformative. It is not a straightforward description of a computer design. So unless you are referring to something that the great Oceanus might have architected it is probably better avoided. There is no need to architect a schedule for a meeting: I doubt the great Oceanus had much time for meetings.

Argument. When you are dealing with an opposing *argument* or the claim of a rival, try to be generous. The temptation to caricature the opposing case needs to be resisted because it sounds churlish. You will not engage a rival if your account of what they are doing is implausible. Customers are too discerning to be taken in, too. If, however, you display the confidence to put the opposing case in a generous way, then you win credibility as a critic once you begin your attack. You win the right to go in harder as you finish because you have been generous at the start.

Audience. All writing is done for an intended reader. Think properly about the expectations and requirements of that reader before you start. In particular, think about how much your *audience* knows about the subject you are addressing. A great deal of business writing is afflicted by the curse of too much knowledge on the part of the writer. This means that the writer has been unable to imagine that the reader does not know as much as they do. The writing, consequently, is dense and hard to follow because things which seem obvious to the writer (but not the reader) have not been cogently explained. Experts who know too much are always tempted by jargon, abbreviations and technical terminology. Remember, though, that most people don't speak this language. They will need taking through your thought process in a more painstaking way. Write for an intelligent person who has no specialist knowledge.

Authentic. A borrowing from existential philosophy which repetition has now wearied. In the philosophical literature, authenticity has the precise sense of knowing oneself and being in control of one's life. Transposed to the arena of business, though, authenticity has a bewildering range of meanings. The term *authentic* is applied to leadership that is stimulating and inspiring, to a successful method of motivating others, to a leader who is aware of his or her own strengths and weaknesses and to one who is true to who they are, whatever that may be. When 'authentic' is applied to a brand the idea becomes even more vaguely capacious. Among its legions of meanings, 'authentic' can mean redeeming a promise, treating customers with respect, ensuring the quality of products, protecting the privacy of customers, acting with integrity, being open emotionally, inviting critical viewpoints, the upshot of trigger events in an autobiography, defining a business purpose beyond profit, being genuine and holding true to your values. Clearly, these are all virtues but all of them are quite specific and separate things. Our understanding of none of them is added to by calling them 'authentic', nor do they add up to something called 'authentic leadership'. All that has happened here is that some business guru has gathered all the usual positive epithets and given it a needless label. Authenticity has been in vogue in the business world since Bill George published *Authentic Leadership* in 2003 and then his 2007 follow-up *True North: Discover Your Authentic Leadership*.

It is a slippery idea whose deficiencies are obvious. Who really knows their true self? It's rather a troubling question and not necessarily one that bears too closely on the task of, for example, running an online price comparison site. Good leadership, in fact, requires a set of attributes that we can specify such as clarity, intelligence and rigour. If your true self includes these attributes, then all well and good. Your authentic self will coincide with someone who is likely to be a good leader. But if your authentic self is not like this, then you are going to have to change. Stubbornly sticking to authentic methods that don't work might be authentic but it is also stupid. It is hard to shake off the suspicion that most people are using the word 'authentic' to mean simply 'good at leadership'. The term is therefore explaining nothing.

If you must use the idea of authenticity, do not stretch the meaning too far. The measure of authenticity is simple. The authentic leader lives up to her words. The brand redeems its promise. It does what it says on the tin. Bear in mind too that we do not want all leaders to be authentic. They might be authentically awful. The best way to cure yourself of excessive use of the word 'authentic' is to remind yourself of all the appalling tyrants, in business and politics, who governed authentically, as themselves. That is always the problem.

Awesome. Be careful with your superlatives. If you say hello by pretending that it is *awesome* to see me, what will you say when I ask if you'd like a coffee? You'll explode with excitement and when I bring you a granola with berries, you'll have no words.

B

B2B. Fine if you need a shorthand when you are talking to people who know what you mean. But remember that most people don't know what *B2B* means and think it sounds stupid when they find out. 'Is that a bit like Air BnB?' The same goes for B2C and all cognate terms. It's not that much of an imposition to write out the words. Better still, find a variety of expressions.

Basically. A throat-clearing word which rarely adds anything. 'Basically, just be a perfectionist about the product you make or the services you provide,' as Elon Musk said.[7] Mr Musk is usually an intriguing speaker, but not this time. *Basically*, try not to use it. Or: try not to use it, as I might have written.

Base. Used *passim* in constructions such as 'our customer base' by which you mean your customers. The BT 2020 annual report is a typical example: 'the size, scope and breadth of our customer base gives us an advantage when new propositions and services are brought to market'.[8] Perhaps this might mean the sort of people who tend to be your customers (rather than the actual group of people who, in fact, are at the moment). The customer base of Waitrose differs from the customer base of Asda, by which we mean the social class of people Waitrose are seeking to attract differs from the social class of people who shop at Asda. It is not clear whether you are referring to actual or potential customers. The solution is to apply the term 'customer base' to neither. It is hard to think of an instance in which adding the term *base* as a suffix adds to the meaning.

Behaviours. The perfectly acceptable plural word *behaviour* has gained a stray s in the corporate world. Almost everyone now uses it, following like sheeps. Again, there are precedents. In a poem about the decay of civilized values, W. H. Auden wrote, in November 1934, 'Looking and loving our behaviours pass/ The stones, the steels and the polished glass'. But Auden was notoriously faddish. Even so, his usage sounds better than Cisco from its 2019 annual report: 'For Cisco, Conscious Culture is an inclusive and diverse environment, molded by our beliefs, behaviors, rituals, and principles.'[9] Rituals? That sounds rather sinister. There is some strange behaviour over at Cisco these days.

It may already be too late to prevent the spread of behaviours but, as usual, what seems like an innocuous change of usage conceals a conceptual shift. The singular word *behaviour* implies that this is what we are like. Our behaviour is all of a piece. The plural *behaviours* breaks that down into individual actions. The things we do (our behaviours) add up to what we are like (our behaviour).

Behind the curve. Strictly speaking, you are underneath the curve. It is quite hard to get *behind a curve* and quite hard to envisage where that is on the graph. The more potent objection is that *behind the curve* has become a cliché. When, for example, Mark Ridley of Savills says that Britain is 'behind the curve'[10] in getting back to work, there could scarcely be a more uninteresting way of putting it.

Benchmark. This is another example of a term that was once vivid and visual. For the builders of Greece and Rome a *benchmark* denoted a series of broad marks in the shape of an arrow that were carved vertically into stone. A horizontal cut would be made in the stone and an angle iron inserted to create a 'bench' which would be used for site surveyors to assess the site. The benchmark was originally the vantage point from which a judgement was made, rather than the measure of the judgement itself. Note how a tired word like *benchmark* has been revived by recuperating its visual image. This is a good example of the vitality of pictorial language.

Best in class. There can only be one product that is truly the best in the class. And it is not really true that only the best in the class can thrive. When Andy Main, the global CEO of Ogilvy, says, 'communications is critical when it comes to driving growth and transforming businesses, which is why it is essential for Ogilvy to have a best-in-class public relations and influence business and a cohesive, modern offering',[11] is he really saying that the market is a monopoly? Of course he is not saying anything so precise. He is expressing a general desire to be very good in a phrase that just came ready to hand. He'd like to be the best, as everyone would, but there is no shame, in most markets, in being the third best in the class. Nobody would ever honestly state that as an ambition, which shows that *best in class* is an empty phrase. The same applies to 'best in breed' with the added objection that there is no reason to compare your products to a pedigree dog or a cow at a country show. Both those phrases are used, thoughtlessly, to mean something bland like 'quite good' or 'better than it used to be'.

Bleeding edge. 'Sometimes the cutting edge is the bleeding edge,' said Kristin Dziczek, vice president of industry, labour and economics at the Center for Automotive Research.[12] To which the only viable response is bleeding hell. This is, as Henry Higgins says in *My Fair Lady*, 'the cold-blooded murder of the English tongue'.

Blue chip. Whenever you refer to a blue-chip company you are using a precise image, although the phrase has become so commonplace that we may no longer notice. The *blue chip* was once, in the casino, the one with the highest value. To recover the image is to be reminded that even an investment in a company of such high repute is a gamble, which is close to the opposite of what you are trying to say.

Blueprint. A perfectly good word which has lost its vivid origin. Sir John Herschel (1792–1871) was a renowned astronomer who was also instrumental in some of the earliest experiments in photography, a term whose use he encouraged. Herschel helped to find a way to introduce colour into photography. His insight was to separate white light using a prism. In 1842, Herschel invented the cyanotype which uses the shade of Prussian blue which lends itself to strikingly beautiful photography. This Prussian blue is the origin of the *blueprint*.

Sadly, the term is now over-used and used badly. A *blueprint* is a comprehensive plan and not just something more provisional such as a proposal.

Brevity. There are virtues for which *brevity* can be sacrificed – beauty of expression for one – but brevity is a virtue of its own.

Bricks and clicks. 'Our story again has been one of "bricks and clicks" success,' said Andy Street when he was in charge of John Lewis.[13] This will have sounded so very clever the first time it was said. 'Bricks and clicks. It rhymes!' On second hearing it is irretrievably David Brent. So is the puntastic clicks and mortar.

Builds. As in 'I have read the document which is magnificent in every way and I have a few builds.' There is so much wrong with this. The first thing is that a *build* is not something anyone would ever say outside a business context. We build things, literally like houses and metaphorically like bridges, and to say, 'I can build on what Leopold Bloom just said there' is perfectly sound English. But the things subsequently said are not 'builds'. We do not build with 'builds'. We build with bricks or wood or some other material. So, if you insist on extending the metaphor, you ought to say 'very good bricks' rather than 'very good builds'. That would make you sound ridiculous but perhaps not more ridiculous than you do anyway. But this is not even the most irritating thing about 'builds'. It is the fake bonhomie, the fictitious spirit of collaboration it is pretending to evoke. It is occasionally true that sequential contributions to a conversation build on a point just made but not often and certainly not always. In most cases we take a little of what has been said and bend and twist it to make something different. We discard things along the way, which no good builder can afford to do. Imagine a house construction in which the builder throws away every fourth brick and replaces it. The analogy breaks down instantly because the builder would be replacing a discarded brick with an identical brick. Writing is not like this. When we discard items we replace them with words that are different and better. Or we simply delete them and make the words bunch up tighter. Try building a wall like that. Good thinking is not at all like building either. Thinking is a circuitous process which swirls back on itself and allows for reflection and changes of course. It is not at all like laying bricks on top of one another in the construction of a sturdy wall so the 'builds' of which you are so fond are both ugly and misleading.

Bullet points. The use of *bullet points* can break up a dense text and make it easier to read. Try to ensure though that you always have a line that leads into the bullet points, rather like this one. Then the following maxims are advisable:

- use lower case at the start
- try to keep a single bullet point to a single sentence
- there is no need for semi-colons or full stops, even at the end

C

Capitalization. As a rule, err towards lower case. Proper nouns should take a capital letter but not offices. So 'President Trump' but 'the presidency is a respected office ...' Also, do you have a Tendency to insert capital Letters almost at Random, like Emily Dickinson? Presumably you wish to draw Attention to the capitalized Words. You do, But Not In A Good Way. It is a good idea for a company to have a policy to maintain consistency across its many media. The names and titles of individuals, place names, organizations and titles of published works should be capitalized. Anything else can be lower case. Newspapers differ markedly on this question but you do at least always know what you are going to get. *The New York Times* Seems To Capitalize Almost Everything while *The Times* rarely does, although it can, at times, go a little far in the opposite direction and come over as strangely e. e. cummings.

Catalyst. Usually a fancy way of saying cause. Not that it means 'cause', of course. A chemical *catalyst* provokes a change but remains itself unaltered. This example, from the Santander 2019 annual report, is one of many: 'Understanding that innovation and digital/technological transformation are a catalyst in our business model and strategy, turning the challenges of technology into opportunities.'[14]

Chair. See also the entry on *Gendered Language*. This has become a minefield and, while there is no need to submit to every demand, be aware that you do not want to offend any of your staff or clients. In general and within reason, try to comply with people's demands. Some language is loaded and gendered for no good reason and it is not unreasonable to be asked to avoid it. This is, in fact, an easy instance. There is no loss of meaning when we shorten 'chairman' to 'chair'.

Challenge. A euphemism that sounds bold but has become feeble. To call something a *challenge* makes it less troublesome than to say it is a problem. 'Challenge' implies that the problem has landed mysteriously from outside. A challenge is never your fault whereas a problem is. But some things are problems and we might as well say so.

Cliché. The introduction to the *Economist Style Guide* contains a parody which might sound uncomfortably familiar and which might alert you to some of the *clichés* you may have been using: 'Basically, I would have to begin by kick-starting the economy, on a level playing field, of course, and then, going forward ... we shall have to get networking and engage in some blue-sky thinking to push the envelope way beyond even our usual out-of-the-box metrics.' Or we could devise a more technical version: 'The go-to strategic partner delivering sustainable value-added product solutions and services to the world's top technology businesses.' There are six clichés in that sentence (*go-to, strategic partner, delivering, sustainable, value-added, product solutions*). The effect is to empty the sentence. The reader is barely paying attention by the end. The trouble with declaring that you prize 'operational excellence, organizational capability and value-added product solutions' is that nobody could disagree. Every company would prefer operational excellence to its opposite. When you declare that you are in business to create 'sustainable value', this in no way distinguishes you from every other business, all of which would love to think the same was true. Indeed, if it isn't true, they won't be in business for long. This is what happens when you resort to business cliché. It is not just that what you are saying is standard and stale. You are often not saying anything at all.

Commas. The best way to work out if a *comma* is needed is to read the sentence out loud. When you run out of breath you need a break. Keith Waterhouse put it well: 'It is not the function of the comma to help a wheezing sentence get its breath back.' Either a comma is required to separate the clauses in a single sentence and allow a pause, or a full stop is needed. Use commas in lists too, to separate items. Apart from that, be sparing because punctuation impedes the flow of a sentence. Stephen Pinker has a full treatment of the conventions of using commas well and badly in *The Sense of Style*. The most common injudicious usage in business writing is known as the 'splice' which is the use of a comma to link two thoughts which ought to be separate sentences: 'Our strategy is clear, we are trying to rent deckchairs on the beach for three quid an hour.'

Compensation. Do you really feel so down at work that you need to be compensated for going? Does it not make you feel a little better to know that they are paying you for your trouble? The use of *compensation* is a pointless change in terminology which deletes an idea that makes perfect sense and replaces it with one that makes less sense. There was never anything wrong with pay and other benefits as a way to describe how people are rewarded for their work. And doesn't that verb introduce a nice feeling? To be rewarded is a compliment, to you and to the job. The work is rewarding and you are rewarded. So much better than the vogue term compensation. In the law and in insurance compensation is money paid to someone as a recognition that they have been hurt or because something has been lost or damaged. It is the stock-in-trade of the personal injury litigator. This is the sense that compensation has in popular parlance too. We receive compensation for a loss. Sometimes for a loss for which there can be no true compensation. Why would a corporate HR department want to imply that work involves loss, for which compensation is needed? Work does indeed involve loss – loss of free time, for example, that we might spend doing something more interesting – but why is it in the interest of the company to point this out? Indeed, it actually sounds rather patronising because there are many jobs which are tough and unpleasant and which really do require compensation. They invariably offer low pay and few other benefits. It is almost always the professions in which people are indulgently wittering on about 'compensation'.

Competencies. The idea of being competent has been broken into parts. This is, for most people, demotion. I would rather be thought competent than to have my *competencies* specified, which rather draws attention to all the missing items on that list, which must be my deficiencies. Maybe we could call them my core brilliances. That last phrase sounds comical but it is exactly the same idea as core competencies.

Complexity. Try to avoid your language becoming too complex, even when you are describing *complexity*. For example, an Accenture executive declared that 'with the rise of the multi-polar world, the task of finding and managing talent has become more complex, turbulent and contradictory'. Turbulent? Contradictory? What contradictions, rather than difficulties, are there in recruitment? This is an attempt to make the structure of the sentence live up to the complexity of the task. But words have precise meanings so that complex ideas can be conveyed succinctly. Try to keep the structure of your thought simple too. If your 8 problems map onto 7 strategic priorities which in turn generate 9 intervention opportunities each of which suggests 5 policy scenarios, then your thinking needs to be simplified.

Confusion. Sometimes we mistakenly write one word for something else which is annoyingly similar. Look out for *adverse* (hostile) and *averse* (disinclined), *affect* (insincerity) and *effect* (make happen), *ambiguous* (susceptible of more than one interpretation) and *ambivalent* (hard to decide between options), *apprise* (tell) and *appraise* (judge), *compliment* (nice to hear) and *complement* (an accompanying thing), *credible* (believable) and *credulous* (gullible), *depreciate* (fall in value) and *deprecate* (disparage), *flaunt* (show off) and *flout* (disobey), *fulsome* (insincere flattery) and *full* (complete), *mitigate* (lessen the impact of) and *militate* (to make something less likely), *opportunism* (making the most of a chance) and *opportunity* (the chance itself), *reticent* (shy and restrained) and *reluctant* (frightened to act).

Consult and meet. There is no need to consult with or meet with, though this is more standard usage in the United States.

Content. These days every second person has the term *content* in their title. If you are not a Content Manager, then you will be a Content Creator, Producer or Designer. Content is written, devised, translated, edited and overseen by Content Specialists and Content Executives. There are Content Builders, Distributors, Officers and Coordinators. Getting vaguer and vaguer (jobs without real content) there are Content Moderators and Content Platform Creators. All overseen by the Head of Content. Maybe a feudal hierarchy should be established. Baron Content. The Count of Content.

In *A Shropshire Lad*, his signature poem, A. E. Housman writes, 'Into my heart an air that kills/ From you far country blows/ What are those blue-remembered hills? What spires, what farms are those?/ That is the land of lost content ...' Unless you are quoting Housman, which is laudable but unlikely, try not to use the word content. It is a fashionable vagueness which tries to cover everything from internal memoranda to television programmes. You might say that it has lost all content.

Couplings. Some words always turn up with a companion. The effect is to deaden the impact of what might originally have been a productive *coupling*. But heat which is always stifling and cold which is always biting should be treated with scepticism which is itself always healthy.

Customer-centric. Trying to speak warmly of a new recruit, Søren Hagh, the European president of Heineken said that 'his authentic leadership style, customer-centric approach and passion for developing talent are a great fit with Heineken as we continue our journey as Britain's leading pubs, cider and beer business'.[15] A business that is not *customer-centric* will go out of business. A business that is customer-centric can let its success speak for itself, which given this awful language is just as well. There is no need for the suffix -centric, except in concentric which does not mean 'focused on deception'.

Customer journey. It is no longer enough simply to buy something. A customer needs to go on a journey, like Odysseus.

D

Data. Using *data* well, to tell a story, is difficult. The best approach is the most radical. In his August 1940 memo Winston Churchill offered the best advice: 'If a report relies on detailed analysis of some complicated factors . . . those should be set out in an appendix.' Leave the text itself as free of clogging numbers as possible. If some data does need to be included in the main body of a report, have the confidence to use the most telling number and only that number. A definitive fact is no more definitive if it is followed by a further seven numbers making essentially the same point slightly less well.

Dates. The custom in most of the world is to begin the week on a Monday so that is probably the best policy. Try to avoid using numbers to represent months because they tend to look messy in print. For example, use 16 May 2020 rather than 16/5/2020.

Deep dive. It sounds like great fun to do a *deep dive* into the data. This is nicely alliterative but all you mean is that you intend to analyse the data properly. Would you ever say we should do a shallow dive into the data? No, so spare me the depth of the dive. But, without the alliteration of deep it sounds awful to say we are going to dive into the data. The data suddenly sounds like a swimming pool. Dismantling the phrase like this shows that it doesn't really work. The attempt to make the work sound fun shows that you secretly think it is boring. You can be more confident than this. Analyse the data well, find the story within it and it will not be boring. Numbers have patterns and their own kind of art and beauty. Anyone who has enjoyed working with numbers knows this pleasure. There is no need to fake it.

Deliver. This is a word that has either crept into business through politics or into politics through business. Either way, it is a metaphor that started as dull and has by now become irritating. Is *deliver* really the best word in the following sentence from the 2019 Huawei report: 'We help app developers deliver innovative app experiences to 600 million Huawei device users around the world.'[16] Would 'create' not have been better? Try to use the word appropriate to each instance. If you are referring to a promise, say that it has been kept rather than it has been delivered on. Improvements are made and public services are provided. The best way to remember this is the story often told by Alan Johnson, the former postman who became Home Secretary. Mr Johnson liked to brag that he was the only Labour minister who had ever really delivered anything. There is another problem with the metaphor of delivery. Sometimes you read that we are delivering the strategy and sometimes you read that the strategy is delivering results. How can you tell the postman from the post, as Yeats might have written, if he had ever done any stanzas on corporate language.

Deliverables. Really? As a Unilever spokesman said, 'We will closely assess the platforms' deliverables against their timelines and commitments, as well as polarization in the social media news feed environment post-election as the year progresses.'[17] I hope the Unilever spokesman had a lie down after that. When the presents you have ordered online turn up do you gather the family around the hearth and declare 'the *deliverables* have arrived'. Maybe you do. Maybe you send Father Christmas a note with the deliverables you expect him to bring down the chimney.

Digitize. Be careful not to use too much. Everyone is *digitizing* and it no longer sounds like the future arriving. Also, remember that digitization is only a new method of delivery. It is not usually the product itself. Be careful you don't spend all your time discussing the means at the expense of the ends.

Disintermediate. This is a road crash pile-up which seems to be assembled from the wreckage of broken words. Reoverformulate. Desuprapostulate. This is also one of those words which sounds precise but isn't. Your audience will hear different meanings and you can avoid the confusion by saying what you actually mean. *Disintermediate* was first used in banking in 1967 and all it meant was cutting out the middle-man. When Peter Kern, the CEO of Expedia, says, 'Google tried to disintermediate us'[18] he means that Google tried to kill his business by making it unnecessary, like water pipes disintermediating the walk to a well with a bucket.

Distinctive. If you have to tell me that something is *distinctive*, then it won't be.

Drive the business. But then we speak of business drivers. Maybe the drivers are *driving the business* but you mean that you are. Then speakers like to introduce strength and direction. As Arjen

Kraaij, the deputy CEO of TIP, said, 'I am honored and excited to take on this new role and work closely with all regional VPs to strongly drive the business forward.' You don't drive strongly. Let's change the metaphor, not least because it is so common.

Dynamic. One of those words, like passionate, which it is better to be than to say. Others should refer to your dynamism. It sounds rather forlorn and needy, rather like saying how good-looking I am.

E

Edit. There are three parts to writing, of which writing itself is the least important. Before writing comes thinking and after writing comes *editing*. Ruthless editing is the road to brevity. The magician Arnold Furst pioneered a trick which has become an editing parable. Furst would scribble the words 'Fresh Fish Sold Here Today' on a long roll of paper. He would tear word by word until the paper was in bits. To the wonder of all, he would then reassemble it. It is a fine old trick but, as a piece of editing, unnecessary, because the sentence was too long to start with. In his book *Newsman's English*, Harold Evans, the former editor of the *Sunday Times*, includes a story which is a journalistic staple. Picture the window of a fish-shop in which the fishmonger has hung a sign which reads, exactly as Furst's roll of paper, 'Fresh Fish Sold Here Today'. A pedantic visitor passes the shop and persuades the fishmonger he has no need of the word 'Today' as this is a tautology. Fish that is fresh will have to be sold today or else it will not be fresh. Then he realizes that the word 'Here' is redundant as nobody who is not here can read the sign and anyone who is here doesn't need to be told. The sign now reads 'Fresh Fish Sold' but the visitor points out that 'Sold' is redundant because he knows that a fishmonger sells fish. Nobody standing outside the window will imagine they could come in and borrow the fish. It's not a fish library. Then, with the sign reading 'Fresh Fish', the visitor makes a more subtle point. To advertise fish as fresh may undermine the intended message. Insisting that this batch is fresh might lead the customer to think that the rest of the produce is not. So, with the word 'Fresh' deleted the sign reads, simply, briefly and precisely: 'Fish'. This seems silly, though. Do you really want a sign that says 'Fish' over a rather obvious display of fish? Certain that the context supplies all the necessary information, the visitor scrubs the sign clean. It shows how brutal you can be. So, when you think you are done, see if you cannot tighten it further. Set yourself the target of shrinking the word count by 10 per cent. The best writing is editing.

Emojis. ☹.

Envisioneer. There is no proscription against making up words. Shakespeare couldn't stop (see the entry on *Neologisms*). The rule, though, has to be that the new coinage is intriguing and adds to the stock of available meaning. This one doesn't. It doesn't work because nobody really talks about 'envisioning' something in the first place. You mean they have seen the future. You mean they are seer or a prophet. And we already have words for that, which will do nicely.

Euphemism. There are plenty of famous examples. Document-management at Enron, enhanced interrogation at the Pentagon. We no longer sack anyone, we 'downsize' or 'rationalize' or 'rightsize'. Presumably, before we 'rightsized' we were 'wrongsize', but nobody would ever say that. Sometimes the euphemism gets out of control. In 2013, HSBC described the firing of 942 as 'demising' them. It's one thing to be down-sized, another to be fired, but worse surely to be killed. This all derives from moral cowardice, from a desire to cover up unwelcome news. It never works. People find out the truth soon enough so tell it straight.

Examples. Strings of abstract nouns could be so much better with the inclusion of a single, illustrative *example*. A point embodied in an image is worth an infinite array of abstract nouns.

Exclamation marks. Should not be used at the end of boring sentences like this one!!!!!! An *exclamation mark* is a once-in-a-lifetime event unless you are reporting a visit to Westward Ho! or quoting a title such as *Look, Stranger!*

Execute. 'We executed well in fiscal 2019, delivering strong top-line growth and profitability,' says the Cisco 2019 annual report. There are so many *executions* going on in some corporate documents that it sounds like Tyburn, *circa* 1836. It is usually only a strategy being executed but at least some of them would be better carried out. You are a corporate manager, not Robespierre.

Experience. Added to the end of a sentence (the attention to detail really enhanced the customer experience) to make something ordinary sound like an existential event. An *experience*, when the word is used appropriately, should leave a lasting mark. The flaw in most corporate usage is that the experience doesn't matter enough. A plastic glass of soda won't necessarily change my life just because you have labelled it an experience.

Indeed, the obligatory use of the word experience in marketing often diminishes the event in question. Take an example such as 'We believe that human relationships require prioritized investment in shared experiences'. Which presumably means that they will organize an office party at Christmas or a weekend away in the Lake District. The strange abstraction 'the customer' also implies that every customer will experience the same thing. It would be an exhausting life if we had an experience every time the vegetables were delivered. (Vegetables, unlike promises, are delivered but it really is just a delivery and not an experience.)

F

False ranges. It sounds euphonious and clever to write something like 'over time they sold everything, from screwdrivers to washing-up liquid'. But a moment's reflection shows you that this is a *false range*. There is no spectrum that runs from screwdrivers to washing-up liquid. If you were to fill in the intermediate values in the range, what would they be and in what order? Hubcaps, plectrums, thimbles and toothbrushes, perhaps? Is that the right order of progression? The answer, of course, is that the range is, in fact, ridiculous. The writer does not mean that it is a genuine progression from screwdrivers to washing-up liquid. The sentence tells us nothing concrete about what they sell (apart from screwdrivers and washing-up liquid). All it says, really, is that this company sells all manner of unrelated stuff. It would be better to offer a list of five or six items for sale and make it plain that there is plenty more where that came from.

Feedback. A boring, ubiquitous work word you would never use at home. 'How is your breakfast?' 'It's nice, thank you, though I prefer my eggs harder.' 'Thank you for that feedback.' *Feedback* is a term which has a precise technical meaning in writing on electrical science. The first usage comes from 1919, from *Improvements in or Relating to Electrical Signalling*: 'The secondary 20 of the transformer is connected by a feedback circuit 21 to the primary 16 of a transformer 15.'

Fractions. Do not mix up *fractions* and decimals in the same sentence because even for numerate readers it can be hard to retain the correct order of magnitude.

Full-service solutions provider. Think of the implicit promise here. We can solve everything you throw at us. It won't be true, inevitably, and we all know it. So what we hear instead is: we will promise too much but we will do what we can. If its meaninglessness isn't enough to persuade you to desist, how about the fact that you sound just like everyone else? Type this into Google and see how many other companies you can find that say the same thing. It doesn't sound so clever all of a sudden. Listen to this absurdity from Shawn Handrahan, the CEO of Valet Living: 'I would like to thank the Ares Private Equity team and Harvest Partners for their invaluable support and guidance over the last five years as we grew Valet Living from a doorstep waste management company to a full-service solutions provider that serves communities across the country.'[19] Where once his company did something useful – taking waste from the doorstep – now it is going to do something useless like solving everything and nothing. *Full-service solutions provider* also fails the test of the absurd opposite. Nobody would ever say that they will fail to solve your problems and that illustrates how banal it is to say that you will.

Future-proof. Nothing is. When John Neal, the CEO of Lloyd's says, 'We have to future-proof the Lloyd's marketplace, not to produce a satisfactory return in 2021, but to produce a sustainable, long-term profitable path for the benefit of all market constituents,'[20] he really only means they should plan for the future as best they can. He knows very well, as a veteran of volatile markets, that if he genuinely had the ability to set up proofs against future uncertainty there would be no capital markets for Lloyd's to trade in. It's not only nonsense, it's self-harming nonsense.

G

Game-changer. An import from American sport and a perfectly vivid and clear one too (see the entry later on *Sport*). The problem is not the phrase but over-use and inappropriate use. *Game-changer* was first used in a business context in 1993 and, over nearly three decades, it has become a cliché. A genuine game-changer alters the course of events for good. Indeed, in bridge, from which the term derives, the 'game-changer' actually changes the game itself, not just the result. You can breathe life back into the metaphor of the 'game-changer' if you use it in this sense, as an event which alters the way others will play the game, an event that changes the rules. It is not just the moment that you played the game well and assured yourself of victory. We should be able to look back and see that this was the pivotal moment, the point from which the conclusion followed. It's not the sort of phrase you can adequately use if someone has a mildly intriguing idea.

Gendered language. The United States Declaration of Independence states that 'all men are created equal'. It ought to be read with the assumption that the word men refers also to women but that is not to say that we should copy the practice. To refer to a professional position invariably as 'he' is wrong. Not grammatically wrong but socially and morally wrong. The codes of language often erase people from consideration and so it is wise, as well as common courtesy, to be sensitive to this fact. Most gendered terms have acceptable neutral alternatives (man/person; mankind/humanity, policeman/police officer and so on). The thorniest issues may arise over the use of the gender pronouns. This is less of a problem in English than it is in languages in which words are either preceded by a gendered preposition (*la vie en rose*) or take a gendered ending (Latino) but it still matters. It is lazy to use 'he' when not all people referred to are male. Using 'he or she' is reasonable, although a bit cumbersome. Some writers alternate genders at random although that is a tactic that rather draws attention to itself. Perhaps the neatest solution is to use 'they' as a singular pronoun. English does, as it happens, have a gender-neutral pronoun and it is not true, as the grammar purists often assert, that 'they' is ungrammatical. It is, in fact, perfectly acceptable English.

Constables from the Grammar Police may try to have you

arrested but using 'they' for 'he or she' has a noble heritage. In the King James Bible, the Gospel of Matthew has 'If ye from your hearts forgive not every one their trespasses'. Chaucer and Shakespeare use the same locution. You can find it in Swift, Byron, Thackeray, Wharton, Shaw and Auden. Jane Austen, who used 'they' regularly, writes in *Mansfield Park*: 'I would have everybody marry if they can do it properly'. Indeed, the use of 'they' and 'their' was standard English in the Victorian era. A celebrated recent usage, which attracted the scorn of the Grammar Police, came from Barack Obama. In a press release in 2013, President Obama praised the decision of the Supreme Court to strike down a discriminatory law with the gender-neutral claim that 'no American should ever live under a cloud of suspicion just because of what they look like'.

If, even with the endorsement of President Obama, you still feel uncomfortable with 'they', or if the sentence really is about an individual which makes the use of 'they' seem strange or impersonal, there are a couple of tricks that avoid the issue. Instead of writing 'every banker deserves their bonus' you could say instead 'all bankers deserve their bonus' or you can make the sentence more generic by saying 'all bankers deserve a bonus'. (Never mind for the moment that it's not true.) But there is no special need to use either of these tricks. 'They' really is fine.

Global language. Lots of business writing reads like it has been written by someone whose first language is not English, even when it is. The best writing is precise and specific and yet much business writing has to be comprehensible across nations that speak different languages and have different cultural expectations. Try to be as locally precise as you can be but here are some tips for writing in a way that will carry across cultures and will make sense to people whose first language is not English. The requirement to write for a global audience makes the point of this book even more forcefully. It is even more important to be clear. Use simple constructions and short sentences. Try to limit the range of your vocabulary; it might be better to use a single term rather than plenty of synonyms, as one might in a more literary piece of writing. Tabulate information where possible. Sentences in the active voice are easier for non-natives to follow. Make a concession to your audience by avoiding idioms and references that are specific to a time and a place. The online audience in Spain might not know the work of Laurel and Hardy. The British might stumble over Michael Jordan. Asking for a piece of work by the close of play might be lost on the Americans whose cricket knowledge is not all it might be.

Global spellings. Proper nouns, such as the names of cities, often have a local name and a name in English. Some common

English words are spelt differently in the United States. There is no rule for how you handle this but try to publish a guide to spread a consistent approach.

Going forward. Time only travels in one direction, as far as we know. There is a brilliant passage in Kurt Vonnegut's *Slaughterhouse-Five* in which time travels backwards, a conceit that Martin Amis borrows in *Time's Arrow* to make a point about moral responsibility. In the world of business time travels forward as a matter of course and there is no need to remind us. There is another way that George Guarini, the CEO of United Business Bank, might have said, 'the business model of banking will be tested going forward'.[21] He could have just said the business model will be tested. The idea that he is talking about time to come is contained in his future tense. The word 'will' has said 'going forward' so that you don't have to.

H

Headings. One way to find the thread of a complex argument is to give each paragraph a heading. Then read the *headings* out loud. If they tell your story, then your argument will flow. If they don't, they will suggest the necessary re-ordering. You are also likely to discover repetitions.

Headwinds and tailwinds. Business executives love *headwinds* and *tailwinds*. It is probably the most common metaphor around that is rarely, if ever, used in any other field. As always with such metaphors there is nothing wrong with it, when used well. Over-use has turned headwinds and tailwinds into clichés, especially when applied with no respect to the metaphor. So, for example, the Reckitt Benckiser 2019 Annual Report contains the flat phrase 'RB operates in strong structural growth categories with an outstanding collection of trusted market brands that benefit from the tailwinds of global mega-trends'. Do global mega-trends (horrible phrase anyway) really have a wind behind them?

Historic and historical. Misused routinely in financial markets. For something to be *historic* it needs to be notable. The Gettysburg Address was historic. It is also an *historical* event because it happened in the past. Previous prices of a stock are historical but they are rarely historic not least because they are too fleeting. Calling them 'historical' reveals the banality of the point you are making so whenever the word springs to mind it might be a sign that the sentence needs to be reconstructed.

Holistic. Usually used to mean that there appear to be a lot of factors and they all seem to be linked in some incomprehensible fashion. Call something *holistic* and absolve yourself from any further need for analysis. To think holistically is to think about everything at once which is, in fact, the opposite of analysis which means to break an idea into its parts. To think holistically is therefore barely to think at all but to provide a lazy and smart-sounding excuse for not thinking, as in this McDonald's statement: 'This year, under new leadership, we have renewed our commitment to values and launched a holistic business plan to drive our future growth.'[22] The word holistic can be withdrawn from this sentence without loss of meaning and with an accompanying gain to credibility.

Hyperbole. Try to be sparing in the use of words that tend to make a melodrama out of ordinary events. *Shock, bombshell, crisis, scandal, sensational, controversial, fury, panic* and *chaos* are all in this category.

I

Iconic. This is a twenty-first-century favourite on which time needs to be called. Since 2001 the usage of *iconic* has increased more than fourfold. Among the many possible examples, what about Zhao Ming, CEO of the Chinese smartphone brand Honor, who aims, he says, to build 'A global iconic technology brand'. Ed Nielsen, the CEO of Whataburger, announced his appointment with the thought that 'it is my honour to be named CEO of this iconic brand'. John Chen, who was brought in as CEO of BlackBerry in 2013 to turn the company around, referred to it superlatively as 'a very iconic company'. With most business usages of *iconic* the speaker really just means 'famous'. The original idea, of pertaining to an image, a figure or a representation has long since fled. But though there is no need to confine the use of the word *iconic* to the history of art, most usages do not meet the modern metaphorical test either. *Iconic* in its recent sense refers to an event or a person or a brand which is in some way representative of a cultural movement or moment. It is not just well known; it is a representative of a notable kind. That might conceivably be allowed of BlackBerry but it's really stretching the case to apply *iconic* to Honor and even more so to Whataburger.

Ideation. A new word for the process of having ideas. Which back in the old days before *ideation* used to be called thinking. Perhaps we could go back to thinking. For the moment we will have to put up with head-scratchers such as this from Rajat Taneja, the president of technology at Visa: 'Social experiences, like a meal or drink together, are hard to have on video. So for me and my team, I think we will have travel but it will be for unstructured work that requires more presence, more ideation and more energy from each other.'[23] I think he is inviting me out to Pizza Express to chat about work but it is hard to be sure and I certainly don't want to go.

Impacted on. Plenty of nouns have become verbs and now sound quite natural. That's not the objection. The objection to *impacted on* is that it is ugly and it is vague. It would be far better to give a sense of the scale of the impact. In this form all it says is that x collided with y and had a consequence of which we can say nothing. Is it a large impact or small? Can we absorb the impact or will it crush us? Is it a nudge or a smack in the face or somewhere in between? We have scales of impact for a reason and you are declining to specify the consequences when you refer generically to the impact. It would be like saying something 'had an outcome'. Well yes, but what outcome?

Ian Grabiner, the CEO of Arcadia, recently said that 'the impact of the Covid-19 pandemic, including the forced closure of our stores for prolonged periods, has severely impacted on trading across all of our brands'.[24] Note the lazy repetition. The impact has impacted on. The rain has rained on us. Actually, Mr Grabiner is not even that precise. Rain is an exact event which made us wet, which was bad. *Impacted on* could, at least in theory, be good. The sun impacted on us in a pleasing way. It is obvious from the context that trading has declined as a result of Covid-19 and it is strangely coy not to say so directly.

Incentivize. It is clear what this means but it is hard to write a euphonious sentence which includes the word *incentivize*. In most cases the writer means no more than 'we will do something to encourage', as in this example from the 2019 BT annual report: 'We've introduced a clause in new BT customer contracts to incentivise the return of products and thereby reduce electronic waste.'

Innovation. In his 1597 essay *Of Innovations*, Francis Bacon wrote, 'As the births of living creatures, at first are ill-shapen, so are all innovations, which are the births of time.' It is a fine word, with a clear meaning, which has been made ill-shapen by poor usage. *Innovation*, as Bacon says here, should imply that there is something novel afoot, not merely that change is likely. When Sindar Pichai says of Google's parent company Alphabet, that 'I think they always envisioned being able to innovate with the structure',[25] he means no more than that it was always likely to change. The word innovation could now do with some innovation itself. Sometimes it sounds like innovation is the holy grail of corporate life. But remember that not all innovative things are therefore wonderful. You can innovate and fail, so try not to use innovation as a vague synonym denoting, in an insipid and general way, 'good' and 'the future'. Nobody ever says, 'We innovated and it was rubbish; I wish we'd just carried on doing the same old thing' but they should. Innovative is also one of those words on which people find it hard to agree on pronunciation. Some people stress the first syllable and some the second. The best option is not to say it at all.

Inputs and outputs. Jargon terms which are usually better replaced with the exact items you are referring to. Nobody will ever stop you, as you are setting out the detailed consequences in the appropriate unit of measurement, and demand that you recast your conversation using the words *inputs* and *outputs*.

Intensifiers. When someone begins a sentence with the phrase 'to be really honest' they invite you to suppose that, the rest of the time, they may well be lying. The same effect comes from the attempt to inflate language with the unnecessary use of *very*, *highly* or *extremely*. As soon as you use *very* you are implying a position high up on a scale of measurement. Is that really what you mean? Is being very honest, rather than merely honest, even meaningful, let alone better?

Interesting. Is very rarely *interesting*. If your sentence is interesting I have already come to that conclusion before your instruction arrives. Likewise if it isn't.

Interface. Is it possible to conceive of a less elegant way to suggest a connection or a meeting? Words like this are markers of the desire of business to become science. *Interface* sounds like a refugee word from an old television show about inventions of the future: 'and now a multi-media inter-face loud-speaker in all-round sound vision'. It sounds so old-fashioned, somehow, when it refers to meeting people. A customer interface sounds like you think customers are aliens. Either that, or you are.

Issue. Like *problem*, *challenge*, *question* and *situation*, this is a boring word that should be replaced and specified where possible.

Iterate. Elon Musk said recently that SpaceX has built ten Starship prototypes and SN9 was developed in parallel to SN8 in order to build 'successive generations of prototypes rapidly so they can test and iterate quickly'.[26] This is just an attempt to make doing something again sound cool. And if iterate means do it over and over, what does re-iterate mean?

J

Jargon. The philologist Wilson Follett called jargon 'mere plugs for the holes in one's thought'. Here is a tip for avoiding jargon, which is a cardinal obligation of good business writing. Write down, on a large piece of paper, every word you might use at work that you would never dream of using at home. Then tear it up and never use any of these words again. Everybody will thank you. See *Part One: The Virtue of Clarity* for a fuller treatment of this avoidable but common error.

Jump. The list of things on which you might *jump* is long. A bed, a pommel horse, a sandpit, for example. A call is not one of them. You don't sound informal, casual and fun. You sound mid-Atlantic, wannabe and weird.

K

K. A thousand. It looks messy in a text and it is clearer to use the number. The same applies to M and B for million and billion.

Key. The 2019 Huawei annual report claims that 'Huawei is committed to long-term investment in *key* technologies while actively contributing to standardization'. This is an almost meaningless sentence which also raises the question of how many things can be *key* all at once? Three, at most, and even that is pushing it. If there are three or fewer key points you could just make them. The very fact that you have selected these points and not some others releases you from the obligation of describing them as key, a useful word that can be reserved for turning locks or for a geographical location in Florida.

L

Last. Try not to use this to mean simply the latest in a series. The 'last announcement at an airport' sounds like a disaster is about to unfold. Perhaps, if it was just the latest announcement, there is no need to hurry.

Learnings. This is a word which makes the user feel so terribly clever and technically accomplished. Drop *learnings* into an ordinary sentence and just hear the crowds gasp. Though this has became an awful contemporary buzzword, learnings in fact has a classical pedigree. 'The king he takes the babe,/ To his protection, calls him Posthumus Leonatus,/ Breeds him and makes him of his bed-chamber,/ Puts to him all the learnings that his time,/ Could make him the receiver of; which he took,/ As we do air, fast as 'twas minister'd', as Shakespeare writes in Act 1 of *Cymbeline*. If you can use it as well as this, then all well and good. But no corporate leader can. Instead, we get Tim Cook, CEO of Apple, saying, 'All of these learnings are important. When we're on the other side of this pandemic, we will preserve everything that is great about Apple while incorporating the best of our transformations this year.'[27] Learnings is a different case from behaviours because it is not simply a change to the plural. Learnings, in fact, means something different to learning. Learning is both the process of acquiring knowledge and the full panoply of your scholarship. Learnings are the individual items you have learnt. You could just as well say 'what I learnt' or 'my lessons' and not a make a fetish of them with the ugly term 'learnings'. It is inconceivable why anyone would ask 'what were your learnings?' rather than 'what did you learn?' Take this as a lesson.

Leverage. This vastly over-used word does, in fact, have a specific and useful meaning. It is the American term for what English financiers call gearing, which is to say the relationship between debt and equity in a corporate structure. There is no ordinary equivalent for that relationship (and no great need for one either) so *leverage* used correctly is a useful addition to a technical vocabulary. Used as a metaphor, however, it adds nothing apart from a failed desire to sound grand. In this context 'use' or 'exploit' or 'deploy' would be better. 'We believe', say BAT in their 2020 strategy report, 'in a multi-category strategy to better meet consumer needs and leverage our scale', which is more or less the same as saying they believe in nothing at all.

Literally. A word that is rarely used *literally* and even when it is tends to be redundant. There is no need, for example, to say, 'I literally coughed' unless there is something unusual and unexpected about your coughing. Most usages of the word literally are figurative, which is to say that it is used when the action in question is not being performed literally at all. So, for example, 'I literally split my sides laughing'. This is a common hyperbole and everyone knows what you mean but it is not an elegant construction and it reveals that you are not really giving your writing careful thought. It's a usage that shows up the kind of writer you are, which is a careless one.

Loop. As in 'I am looping in Jeremy here'. Does Jeremy feel looped in, I wonder? It might be nice to feel included every now and then instead.

M

Margin. Be careful what you claim to be doing with the *margin*. If you find yourself moving the margin forward, your metaphor has slipped its moorings. You need to increase the margin. It needs to go up, not forward. You see a rise, not an uptick (see *Uptick* below).

Matrix. The word *matrix* brings intriguing connotations. In ancient Rome, a matrix was a female animal kept for breeding, or a plant (sometimes called a 'parent plant' or 'mother plant') whose seeds were used for producing other plants. In Middle English, 'matrix' was a synonym for a mother's womb. A matrix has a precise mathematical usage, which is the point of transfer into business writing. Very few corporate users have the echoes of any of these usages in mind. For most contemporary speakers, matrix refers either to a bad film or a desire to be pretentious. Witness, for example, the following, from Santander's 2019 annual report: 'Based on this materiality assessment, a materiality matrix has been generated, where 15 material issues for the Bank have been identified as the most relevant issues.'

Meaningless words. There is no need to mock one more time the dreary instances of *meaningless words* and phrases. You know the sort of phrases. Boil the ocean and so on. Try to replace every one with an image that makes visual sense. For example, you often read in business prose of self-correcting networks. This probably means that a market economy, when it works well, is a network of relationships in which the good is served without conscious intent. In other and better words, by the operation of what Adam Smith called 'the invisible hand'. Rather than use a bloodless and opaque idea like a self-correcting network, Smith uses a memorable image.

Measures. It is usually better to use the short form for measurements (mph, GDP) but the golden rule is to be consistent. It reads better in written script to write out per cent rather than using % which can get lost in a text but consistency is more important than any particular policy.

Metaphor. In one of his less distinguished moments Samuel Johnson once suggested expelling metaphors from the English language. That would be needlessly limiting. Try to keep control of a *metaphor* by thinking literally about what you are suggesting. So, for example, if your argument has 'four cornerstones' or 'four pillars', try to ensure that the verb matches the metaphor. It makes sense to erect pillars and cornerstones or to lay them or to build them. It does not make sense to navigate them. Cornerstones are, as the clue in the name tells you, not difficult to locate. They do not require much navigation.

Middle East. Different companies mean different countries in the various ways they designate geographical jurisdictions for the business. It is usually a good idea to publish a guide.

Militate and mitigate. Militate does not mean mitigate and mitigate does not mean militate. To *mitigate* something is to lessen its impact; to *militate* against something is to make that thing more difficult. It does not make sense to mitigate against anything. It's an easy one to get wrong. William Faulkner did so in his 1931 short story, *Centaur in Brass*: 'Some intangible and invisible social force that mitigates against him.'

Military metaphors. Probably an even more important source of tough-sounding business talk than sport, perhaps because sport also abounds in military metaphors and passes them on. *Captive market, gaining ground, pre-emptive strike, guerrilla marketing, captains of industry, headhunter, make a killing, the sales force.* But terms like *the front line, call to action, in the trenches* manage to sound both grandiloquent and tired at the same time.

Mission statements. A mission statement, done well, is a short statement of what your company does for its customers, employees and owners. It explains how and why you do what you do and ought to be a document that applies only to you. Bad *mission statements*, of which there are plenty, are undifferentiated and could apply to almost any company. Almost all extant mission statements are some variant on 'It is our mission to continue to authoritatively provide access to diverse services to stay relevant in tomorrow's world' which was generated, cheaply and quickly, by a computer algorithm. Slow, expensive versions are available. Look up Weird Al Yankovic's *Mission Statement*. If that's what you sound like, you need to employ a writer.

The best mission statements are ethical guidelines by which a company is bound. The mission statement of the TED organization reads simply 'Spread ideas'. LinkedIn is less pithy but describes exactly what they do, in simple language: 'To connect the world's professionals to make them more productive and successful'. McDonald's are aiming 'to be our customers' favourite place and way to eat and drink'. But these are the exceptions. Most corporate mission statements fall into pretentious exaggeration and transparent euphemism.

Try not to claim too much. Sony want, apparently, 'to fill the world with emotion, through the power of creativity and technology, and to nurture innovation to enrich and improve people's lives'. Mission statements of this kind usually pile in good intentions as if every business were UNICEF, like this Steve Jobs classic: 'To make a contribution to the world by making tools for the mind that advance humankind.' Someone ought to have told him 'it's just a phone, Steve. You're not Mahatma Gandhi.' Starbucks rather ambitiously sought 'to inspire and nurture the human spirit – one person, one cup and one neighborhood at a time'. Avery Dennison had a mission statement in which they promised 'to help make every brand more inspiring, and the world more intelligent' which is quite the ambition for a company that makes stick-on labels.

Perhaps even more irritating than claiming too much is trying to hide what you are really doing. Try not to copy British American Tobacco who coyly refer to stimulating the senses of adult consumers worldwide rather than mention people smoking cigarettes. BMW never mention cars but tell us instead that they want 'to become the world's leading provider of premium products and premium services for individual mobility'. Space-hoppers, maybe?

Monetize. You mean sell. There is nothing wrong with selling. To turn something into money sounds more vulgar than selling it, not less. The truly skilled and dedicated user though, such as the writer of the 2019 Huawei annual report, can generate something meaningless from the term: 'this enables carriers to monetize experience in addition to bandwidth, improving ARPU by more than 25%'. What they mean is that they want to make people pay for stuff. That is all they mean and it is a good idea, in a business, to make people pay for stuff. Put like that it seems rather starkly obvious. But maybe many of the precepts of business *are* starkly obvious and avoiding this troubling fact might be why annual reports, which are seeking to make something complex out of a simple process, are so often so full of guff like this. In truth, Mr Micawber was right about business: 'Annual income twenty pounds, annual expenditure nineteen and six, result happiness. Annual income twenty pounds, annual expenditure twenty pounds ought and six, result misery.' To pretend there is a lot more to it is to be needlessly defensive because the fact that the objective of a business can be pithily described does not make it easy to achieve. Ronald Reagan once said that politics was simple but hard to do. The same is true of business. Just because it's simple doesn't mean it's easy.

N

Neologism. Eras of great tempest bring with them linguistic change as new terms are invented to describe novel circumstances. Shakespeare was a notable coiner of new words. Among those words we still use, Shakespeare was probably the first source for *accessible, accommodation, addiction, barefaced, champion, characterless, circumstantial, compromise, control, countless, critical, defeat, domineering, employment, engagement, excitement, foul-mouthed, frugal, generous, ill-tempered, import, investment, lacklustre, lament, manager, marketable, money's worth, negotiate, overpay, overview, profitless, retirement, subcontract, successful, supervise, title page, undervalue, unlicensed, unsolicited, valueless* and *watchdog.* Writing well about business would be a lot more difficult if we forswore use of all those. But just to show that language is alive there are also some Shakespearean inventions that we have killed off. We no longer have much use for *bodikins, braggartism, brisky, broomstaff, budger, coppernose, fangled, flirt-gill, keech, kickie-wickie, lewdster, plumpy, skimble-skamble* or *wittolly.* The point is that every new coinage should be judged on its merits, not disdained, or even embraced, simply because it is a novelty. Not every neologism adds to the rich expressiveness of the language, though plenty do. One coinage we might like to revive, for example, is *fat-witted.*

No, not. It has been said that the ability to say *no* is the true mark of good management. It is often the mark of good writing too. A sentence such as 'there was a complete absence of strategy' would be much better as 'there was no strategy' or 'they did not have a strategy'.

Nouns. It is, for the most part, good advice that a noun ought not to be verbed. Once again, however, use your discretion. Turning *nouns* into verbs can lead to ugly coinages such as 'solutioning'. But lots of established verbs began their life as nouns. Bill Bryson has pointed out that *to gossip, to fuel, to preside, to surround* and *to hurt* are all part of the fashion of the late sixteenth century for turning nouns into verbs. We have no problem with the words *look, drink, act, fight, like, sleep* or *blame*, among countless others, that we use routinely as both nouns and verbs. Indeed, some unconventional usages can be intriguing and replete with possibility. Toyota recently offered the advice to 'Start Your Impossible' which, strictly speaking, doesn't make sense but in fact does convey a sense of ambition in a rather evocative way.

Numbers. You will have to include *numbers* in your copy on many occasions. There is no single correct way in which this should be done. Think about it, set a policy, distribute it and police it for consistent use. However, it does tend to look better in a text to write out numbers between zero and nine in full and then use numerals from 10 onwards. I don't know why that should be true, but it just is. There are exceptions to this. If you are enumerating items in a list, for example. If one item takes a numeral, then all the items should. So, for example, it would be better to write 'a book as good as *To Be Clear* takes between 9 and 12 months to compile' rather than 'between nine and 12 months'. If you include a unit of measurement, such as £6, then £6 is better than six pounds, 4 tonnes better than four tonnes. Also, don't start a sentence with a number. Figures over 999 ought to include a comma. It is easier to distinguish 1,000 when reading at pace than 1000. Your aim should be that the numbers you use must be easily understood on a first reading by someone with no specialist knowledge of the subject.

O

Occasion. An *occasion* is a special event but not in the corporate world where it can refer to almost anything. A snacking occasion, for example, by which we mean a bar of chocolate or a meal. This is a word that is, like *experience*, added to ordinary events in the illusory belief that it makes them sound more exciting.

Onboarding. A pointlessly complex and unattractive way to say that you have hired someone who is now going through the process of signing the papers in the HR department and being shown where the coffee machine is and where the loos are. 'It was the kind of onboarding we'd never seen before,' said Daniel Danker, senior director of product, Uber Eats.[28] And let's hope we never see it again. They are *joining* you but perhaps that doesn't sound collegiate enough. To be onboard (always one word, for some reason) implies a shared mission, a common endeavour trapped on a ship at sail on the sea. This is a rather grand metaphor if all you have done really is to join a company that sells photocopiers.

Ongoing. The flow of a sentence should already make it plain whether something is *ongoing* or not. The presence of this word ('currently' is the same, although less ugly) is always a sign that the sentence would be better either reworded or recast. 'Despite the ongoing impacts of Covid-19, with the CVA approved and additional funding in place, we are now able to look to the future with cautious optimism,' said Jacqueline

Gold, the chief executive of Ann Summers.[29] She means that Covid-19 is still a problem.

Opposites. Take the following sentence, of a kind which has appeared in many corporate reports and mission statements: 'We value our people as our greatest asset because they are the key to the profitability we hope to generate in the future.' Then imagine its *opposite*: 'We could not care less about the people who work for us because they don't really contribute much anyway and we would be fine without them.' Or try this one: 'It is important to have highly competent teams with the right people in the right roles, focused on our customers.' The *opposite* of which is: 'It is important to have hopeless teams with all the wrong people in the wrong places and our customers can go hang.' When you have written a bland sentence, bear its opposite in mind. If its sentiment is outrageous, makes you laugh or makes no sense at all, then your writing is empty. A meaningful sentence always has a meaningful opposite, which a rational person might conceivably say and think.

Optionality. As T. S. Eliot once almost wrote, 'human beings can only bear so much optionality'. So too functionality and all species of –ality except personality, which is exactly what these words lack. You mean your options. Optionality is how the robots will speak when they take over. Perhaps they have already if the example of Michael Barry, an investor advising Tesla to issue more shares, is anything to go by: 'You'd be cementing permanence and untold optionality.'[30] If only the optionality had indeed gone untold.

Order. It is often necessary to organize a large body of material. Too many business texts proceed from item to item at random. You need an organizing category so that the reader's progression through the work feels natural. Your category might go from top to bottom or it may take the instances in the *order* they occur in time. You might rank them by importance or by size, the order in which a client might encounter them or by their geographical location. Whatever category you choose you need one and that way you can tame unruly information.

P

Paragraphs. The Fowlers' style guide *The King's English*, offers the sound advice that a good paragraph is 'essentially a unit of thought not of length'. Change the paragraph when you change the subject.

Parallel-path. Used as a verb as in the sentence 'Can you parallel-path designs one and two?' It is examples like this that show some businesses are engaged in a deliberate conspiracy against clarity. We need to fight back with all the simple words at our disposal. In this case, the counter-revolutionary response would be to say, 'Do you think you could do them both at the same time, please?'

Participles. There is, in lots of business writing, a strong and unbecoming fondness for the –ing form. A sentence which is decked out with *participles* creates a distance between the writer and the reader. So, for example, you might write that 'persuasion begins by accepting that it is not about you' is somehow vaguer and more distant than 'persuasion begins when you accept that it is not about you'. The reason the second version works better is that it addresses a person as both the subject and the object of the sentence. The participle makes the relationship abstract. The more direct address reinstates the relationship.

Passive voice. It is often said, with no real justification, that nouns should not be verbed. Far more common, in fact, and much more insidious, is the habit of turning verbs into nouns. As soon as you write 'there is no expectation that' rather than 'I do not expect' you are evading responsibility for the thought. The scholar of the written word Helen Sword calls these constructions 'zombie nouns' because nobody is doing the expecting; it just seems to happen. The *passive voice* always allows you to pretend that you did nothing. It wasn't your fault. Mistakes were made. Just not by me.

Pathfinder. A word that has crept into common usage in public policy as well as in business life. It usually means an experiment or a provisional attempt. If you must use it, at least specify the path you are looking for.

Percentage, proportion. These are precise terms so don't throw them away on imprecise usages. Don't say 'a proportion of the earnings came from Europe'. Specify the proportion or don't say it. Be as exacting with the words as you are with the numbers. The terms *percentage* and *proportion* should almost always have a number attached.

Piece. Attaching the word *piece* to the end of a phrase has become a verbal tic. The strategy piece, the future piece, the information piece and so on. The speaker does not mean they have written an article on the subject. They just mean, respectively, the strategy, the future and the information. None of these instances demands the word *piece*. It may be the strangest redundancy in corporate life. Comic usage, though, should be encouraged. Do talk about the hair piece. Or the cake piece. The make piece, the war piece. You can have hours of fun.

Playbook. 'Our strategy combines this with focused playbooks in each one of the category spaces,' say Reckitt Benckiser in their 2019 Annual Report. *Playbook* is another metaphorical import from the world of sport. A playbook is the volume in which the team's strategy is written down. In most usages, like the one above, it is used to describe the strategy itself. Most people don't know what it means and it is easier to make this simple point in a more straightforward way.

Pretentious diction. One of the blights lamented by Orwell is rife in modern corporate writing. The people at Toyota seem unaware of the useful and well-known word 'car' which they call instead a 'sustainable mobility solution'. Speedo claim to offer not a swimming cap but a 'hair management system' and Nestlé advertised an 'affordable portable lifestyle beverage' known to the rest of us as a bottle of water. This extends to pretentious claims about the world. WeWork, for example, stated as their aim the desire to 'elevate the world's consciousness' as if they were drafting a terrible rewrite of the preface to Hegel's *The Philosophy of Right*. They provide office space and the world needs office space. There is something oddly insecure in these extravagant and bizarre claims. There is nothing wrong with saying you can use our good offices. There, they can have that slogan, if it's not too late.

Proactive. Another coinage, which started life in an obscure academic psychology paper from 1933, which business people find strangely tempting. It probably sounds more scientific and technical than the better words it stands in for, such as *vigorous* and *energetic*, *eager* and *keen*. It can usually be subtracted without loss of meaning, as with this example from the 2019 Huawei annual report: 'In 2019, Huawei made a concerted effort to enhance transparency and communicate more proactively with the world.' George Bernard Shaw once said that the single biggest problem in communication was the illusion that it had taken place. This is a case in point.

Purpose. Every business is now set upon defining its *purpose* in terms that never mention material gain. There is some nobility in this but don't lose sight of Peter Drucker's insight, to which there is no shame attached, that 'there is only one definition of business purpose: to create a customer'.

Purposes. Try to avoid the pointless addition of purpose at the end of a phrase, such as 'for development purposes'.

Q

Qualifiers. A good argument will be muffled and lost if you do not show confidence in it. Go through your prose searching for *almost, apparently, fairly, largely, in part, mostly, partially, possibly, presumably, relatively, seemingly, to some extent* and all other words that lessen the clarity and boldness of the proposition. Strip them all out and see how your argument tightens. Listen to how bold and how clear it has become. Now ask yourself: do you still mean it? Perhaps your excessive use of *qualifiers* is due to your inability to make up your mind. If so, come to a clear decision before you begin to write. Your language is telling us you don't know what you mean, even if you haven't realized it yourself yet.

Quality. This is probably a lost cause because the use of *quality* to mean good is now so common. Even newspaper advertisers, who ought to know better, describe their product as at the quality end of the market. There is no need to be zealous but whenever you are tempted to use *quality* when you mean to praise something, imagine using the word quantity when what you really meant was seven. Perhaps the best argument against quality is that it is a bit vulgar and informal. Introduced into a business context it sounds like bad dressing-room banter.

Quota. This is a word with a precise meaning and that precision is better respected. Sometimes *quota* is used when share or complement would be better: 'The company had its full quota of problems.'

Quotation marks. There are two good reasons for placing a passage, a phrase or a word within *quotation marks*. First, you may be citing someone else who has written or said the words you are quoting. Second, quotation marks can indicate that you do not accept the verdict suggested by the phrase. So, for example, you might write that using gendered pronouns is thought to be 'politically correct' as a way of undermining that judgement.

Quotation marks should not be used, however, to distance the writer from the idiom or, even worse, placed at random around a common phrase. Anyone who writes that the team need to think 'outside the box' is aware that the last phrase is an awful cliché but either too afraid or too lazy to find an alternative. The shudder quotes say, in effect, 'I've said it but I am not really saying it; someone else is'. The phrase is instead attributed to an unidentified anonymous other person. It's an apology for your language. When you are tempted to reach for the shudder quotes reach for the thesaurus instead and say something better.

R

Raise the bar. 'We at Lavazza are honored to partner with Faena who continue to raise the bar in hospitality,' said CEO Davide Riboni,[31] forgetting that he was talking about drinking coffee in bars rather than doing the pole vault or the high jump. Another tired import from the world of sport.

Reach out. A horrible and needless expression for an idea that is adequately covered by the idea of talking to someone or contacting them.

Reading. It is a good idea to read your work out loud. There is nothing as good as hearing your prose spoken for unearthing its repetitions, peculiarities and infelicities. Whenever you run short of breath, punctuate. Whenever you bore yourself, cut. Whenever you say a word you would never usually say, alter your vocabulary. You will find that you have what Martin Amis calls an 'inner ear' which means that you will wince when a sound is repeated too soon. This applies not just to words that have been recently used but also to syllables. Amis cites the example of Vladimir Nabokov's dissatisfaction with the proposed title of his 1938 novel *Invitation to An Execution*. That looks fine but say it. The repetition of –ion and –ion is hard to say. It interrupts the rhythm. That's why the book is instead called *Invitation to A Beheading*. That title is more arrestingly and gruesomely visual but it also just sounds better. Edit your prose out loud and you will be going back to the honourable origins of rhetoric. Isocrates used to instruct his clients that rhythmic lines demanded they avoid a repetition of vowel sounds or a clash of consonants.

Real time. In an interview with Mike Atherton for *The Times*, Nathan Leamon, the England cricket team's data analyst, said that 'we were sending signals to the captain in real time' by which he meant that they were sending signals to the captain. *Real time* is a computing term and, in its original location, has a precise meaning. It describes a process in which a response is guaranteed to a short deadline. Such a process usually takes place in defined instalments, each one of which affects the outcome of the process. It therefore means more than just 'time, as we experience it' or 'you'd better hurry up' which is what most users seem to mean. To the rest of us, real time is known as 'time' and as we live in it, or perhaps through it, all the time, we do not feel the need to refer to it.

Red tape. There are lots of tired phrases that were once vivid and they can be brought back to life now that everyone has forgotten the original reference. *Red tape* is a good example. Is there anything drearier than a business complaining about bureaucracy? Yes, there is. It is a business complaining about bureaucracy and using the tired expression 'red tape'. Yet how much more intriguing might the complaint sound if we reminded the reader that public documents have often been bound in red tape and that the first person to popularize the use of red tape to signify the obstruction and circumlocution of an inefficient state was Charles Dickens. In his early days as a parliamentary sketch writer Dickens received the copies of Hansard bound in red tape and the phrase turned up regularly in his fiction, in *The Old Curiosity Shop*, *Little Dorrit* and especially in the satire of the Court of Chancery in *Bleak House*. Add in some of this and your complaint about regulation is already sounding a little less obviously self-regarding.

Refresh. A euphemism for a new corporate structure which will probably mean job losses. The staff are wise to these euphemisms now. You are only kidding yourself.

Reposition the portfolio. Another euphemism, this time meaning the intention to sell off some businesses and maybe buy some others. As soon as you make this intention stark, the staff will begin to worry that their jobs are under threat. However, you do not allay their anxiety by trying to conceal your meaning in strange words. We have become so accustomed to this kind of talk that we have learnt to translate in a sort of pointless parlour game. What does the following sentence, from Mark Read, chief executive of Kantar, mean? 'We have the ability to grow organically, there's also the opportunity to invest and acquire attractive businesses to reposition the portfolio.'[32] It means we will try to get bigger doing what we do but if we fail we will buy another business and do something different.

Research shows that or *studies show*. Usually better omitted as it always sounds strangely amateur and apologetic. If the research really does show what you suggest, append a footnote or a link to that research and then simply tell us what it says.

Roll-out. Why do businesses that are expanding take their metaphorical inspiration from carpets? Could you not just expand or extend or grow? In fact, this is another sporting metaphor, taken from American football, poker and backgammon though that will be lost on most of the people who use the term. Nothing is ever extended or distributed any more. It is always *rolled out*. 'Since the start of the pandemic we've invested billions of dollars in our safety programmes, including rapidly rolling out onsite COVID-19 testing at our sites,' as an Amazon spokesperson said.[33]

S

Same page. Everyone is always on the *same page*. This is usually taken to mean that we all agree. But it doesn't mean that at all. Let's all turn to the same page of Donald Trump's *The Art of the Deal*. As soon as we start reading, we will agree as long as we stay on the same page, right? No, wrong, we are likely to disagree passionately. And we don't sound very critical or intelligent if all we do is turn to the same page as everyone else and blithely agree on its contents. It doesn't sound like much of a book if we all find the same page and then never read on. Why does nobody ever turn over the page and begin a new chapter?

Scenario. A nice word which started out life in the theatre and the opera and which has been corrupted in corporate life. *Scenario* has become one of those dull words like *position* and *situation* which can often be omitted. For example: 'You'll see a hybrid scenario ... We think 80%-plus of that occupancy, if not more, will come back,' as Bob Sulentic, the CEO of CBRE, said about office working.[34]

Sentence length. Sentences that are far too long are hard to follow. The argument gets lost, and readers give up, if the writer refuses to allow us a break. There is a lot of evidence to suggest that when a sentence exceeds twenty words it gets harder to follow. That last sentence was exactly twenty words long so I was testing your patience and this time I am exceeding it. Break up your writing so that short and long sentences alternate. As well as clarifying your case, this will produce rhythmic writing.

A good sentence has something to tell us, something that needs to be disclosed. That something should be kept to the end because a sentence in which the burden is unloaded early loses all weight towards the end. Stephen Pinker quotes a famous lyrical example of good writing: 'May I introduce to you, the act you've known for all these years, Sergeant Pepper's Lonely Hearts Club Band.' If Paul McCartney had revealed the name first, how many of us would have stuck around to hear the introduction which he would, inadvertently, have made redundant?

Shoot. Guns, footballs, pool, films, dice yes. Emails, no. We lack a precise word for the act of communicating by email which is why grown adults have been known to both write and say the word 'ping'. This is not an acceptable word, even if it is followed by 'pong' because that is a needless denigration of the great game of table tennis.

Show not tell. I do not feel energized because I am told to be so. I need your argument to infuse me with energy (without use of the word 'energized''') rather than merely instruct me. The same is true of the word 'passion'.

Skillset. The word skills are applied to everything these days. Bobby Charlton was good at football but Wayne Rooney had footballing skills. Raheem Sterling probably has a *skillset*. Or to change the profession, Yeats was a good poet, Auden had poetic skills and Simon Armitage can leverage his poetic skillset. The strange compound skillset (which is sometimes two words and sometimes one) usually applies to a collection of things which are barely skills at all but traits or aspects of personality. An example which layers irony upon irony comes from David Solomon, the CEO of Goldman Sachs: 'I'll tell you one that we're finding less and less inside the firm that I think is an important skill set, but actually we find it from students that come from Hamilton or other liberal arts backgrounds, is an ability to write.'[35] Not an ability, on that evidence, that the boss has in any great measure.

Solution. Best left for organic chemists. *Solution* is another generic term that conveys a vague sense of approval and nothing more. The less said about newly minted forms such as 'solutioneering' the better.

Space. *Space* bears a family resemblance to *piece* because it is used in the same way, as an unnecessary book-end to a sentence. The marketing space, the B2B space, the peanut and chips space and so on. It makes you sound like you just arrived from outer space on a space-hopper. In almost all instance the word space is a waste of space.

Sport. Business is not *sport* and there is a limit to what you can learn about business from the experience of having played rugby for New Zealand. The agenda of business away-days shows that many executives are oblivious to the lack of connection. It can be hard to avoid sport on any given day at work. *The ball is in their court, it's all going down to the wire, get it over the line, a knockout blow, on the starting blocks, let's touch base, the level playing field, a ballpark figure, slam-dunk, heads up, playing hard-ball, different ball park, a game-changer, moving the goalposts, pole position* and *curveball*. Yet try to avoid sporting clichés in your writing. They do not contain much insight, they exclude people who do not know about sport and they have become a dull cliché. So no *close of play*, no *sticky wicket*, no *game of two halves*, no *behind the eight ball*.

Stand-alone. This rarely needs to be specified. Make it clear in the context that something stands alone. Check too that it is important that the reader should know this.

Statistic. Do not use as a grander word for number. Be careful too that your desire for statistical proof doesn't make your argument too dense. 'If you torture the data long enough,' said the economist Ronald Coase, 'it will confess.' The temptation to pile number upon number must be resisted. The best argument revolves around the best and most telling number, strategically placed to make the case. A representative story which serves as a parable is more convincing than a didactic assertion.

Steer. As in give me a *steer*. But there is no such thing as a steer. You steer with something, usually a wheel or an oar. So next time you want someone to give you a steer, ask them for a wheel instead. Or an oar. You will sound a bit more ridiculous, but not much.

Strategy. Almost all companies have a *strategy* document and, for a set of papers that share a title, they manage to be both tediously similar and remarkably diverse. The tedious similarity comes from the language which is invariably boilerplate corporate. The diversity is even more worrying because these strategic documents exhibit no clarity at all on what the word strategy might conceivably even mean. Some list the company's objectives, which is to say the things it is trying to do. Sometimes these are general (invest for the long term) and sometimes they are specific (invest in renewable energy). Some documents are an attempt to locate and define the purpose of the company, which is said to be distinct from what they actually do. The words purpose, mission, strategy and vision are all jumbled up and end up as Humpty Dumpty words meaning whatever the speaker wants them to mean.

Style guide. All institutions which care about how their employees speak and write publish a *style guide*. This will serve as a guide to the house style. At their best these documents are permissive rather than dogmatic and their main virtue is that they encourage consistency rather than instructions in correct usage. Some companies have such guides and every company ought to have one. A good corporate style guide would be a mixture of useful general principles of composition and information more specifically tailored to the company in question.

Synergy. The supposed benefits of combination, with an added infusion of energy, like a rebranded drink. Better to specify the benefits and avoid the word. When the benefits remain unspecified the user probably means that two things have something in common, as in this example from Adrian Hallmark, the CEO of Bentley: 'We will have much more synergies with Audi in five to 10 years' time than with Porsche because Porsche is sportier and we are more on the luxury side than the performance side.'[36]

T

Tailwinds. See *Headwinds.*

Takeaway. Best reserved for food taken out in a box. It is a good practice to try to crystallize what you have taken from a meeting but a good speaker will have done that refining and editing for you. So don't suppose as a matter of course that there is only one thing to be taken from every address. Maxine Williams, the chief diversity officer of Facebook, said that 'the biggest takeaway is that the later you start, the harder it is'.[37] Imagine if the great aphorists had ruined their pithy thoughts so efficiently. Oscar Wilde might have said that the *takeaway* here is that I have nothing to declare except my genius. The

Duc de La Rochefoucauld could have said that the takeaway is that our vices and our virtues are the same thing. How silly they were not to realize that their maxims could be so easily improved.

Talent. Now applied to the people you recruit. It is always nice to flatter your audience but if everyone who arrives is the *talent*, the word is drained of all meaning. This habit is even worse in some industries, especially the creative types, where 'the talent', who appear in public, are separated from the worker bees who, by implication, are not worthy of the title.

Tautology. The habit of saying the same thing twice within the same phrase. This offends the principles of brevity and concision. For example, revert back, repeat again, collaborate together.

Technology-enabled. Pretty much everything is *technology-enabled*. Talking on the phone, writing with a fountain pen, making a cup of tea. They are all technology-enabled. You are reading a technology-enabled book. This is one of those general terms which sound scientific but say nothing. Specify the particular technology that is relevant in each case.

Topic. Once you have established the point you want to make – and most of the writing failures that occur in the business world come about because the writer is not, in fact, sure what they want to say – don't hide it. The main point needs to go at the beginning of your address. Don't be tempted to leave the reader or the listener in suspense, awaiting the revelation of your point. You're not Agatha Christie and you are not writing a thriller. The revelation, even when it comes, is unlikely to have been worth the wait. Tell us straight away what you have to say and then deepen it as you proceed. In fact, some of the best thrillers give us all the relevant information at the beginning. Dostoevsky opens *Crime and Punishment* by telling us that Raskolnikov did the deed. The novel is then a thrilling explanation of how and why and the consequences attendant on that deed. Crime and punishment is sadly appropriate for too many business presentations.

Triage. Lends a spurious medical precision to the simple placing of tasks in order of priority. Not wrong as such, just pretentious.

U

Uncertainty. We have heard many times that the one thing businesses hate is *uncertainty*. Not a lack of growth or excessive regulation or high corporate tax rates but the mere prospect that such things might happen. Or might not. Or indeed that something else might happen because, in a time of uncertainty, who can tell? Imagine that we had absolute certainty that, next week, the government will forcibly close down all shops that sell mops and buckets. Would the mop and bucket vendor express his delight: 'Though I face bankruptcy, the thing I hate most is uncertainty and at least that is over'? No, because uncertainty is being used, all the time, in two ways, only one of which makes any sense at all. The first sense is to say that some bad things might happen. This is true but it is always better to specify those looming events that are causing you anxiety. That is what you fear, not the uncertainty around them.

The second sense is worse than that because people often use uncertainty to denote the obvious fact that we cannot predict the future. When did anyone ever say 'we have entered a time of complete certainty'? The future *is* uncertain. It doesn't become more or less so. What you mean is that the possible consequences are worse or that the likelihood of something terrible occurring has increased. When the word *uncertainty* creeps into your head it is always good to ask yourself 'What do I really mean here?' *Uncertainty* is one of those words that have taken over thought and almost always mean less than we at first suppose.

Unique. Think carefully and use sparingly. The chances are that the event, property or capacity you are about to describe as *unique* really isn't. A simple question will ascertain the truth. Is this the only one? Are you the only person? Really, none other, anywhere, like a fingerprint? If so, go ahead; unique is *le mot juste*. But on the assumption that all you really mean is 'rare and very good', let's find a more precise way of saying what you mean. You may mean 'exceptional' or 'unusual' or 'magnificent' or 'only available in this country from us'. Say that. Try to avoid the meaningless comparison of 'more unique'. It would be preferable to preserve the sense that unique really is unique and that sense is diminished if we imply there is a range of uniqueness.

United Kingdom. Businesses are often confused, geographically. The *United Kingdom* has a precise meaning. It refers to Great Britain and Northern Ireland. This is not the same place as Great Britain, which excludes Northern Ireland, and it is different again from the British Isles, which also includes the Republic of Ireland. There is no need to make a fetish of these distinctions but it is important to ensure you are saying what you mean to say.

Upskill. There is a Charlie Brown cartoon in which Snoopy complains that Charlie had promised to teach him French but that he hasn't. 'I promised to *teach* you,' replied Charlie, 'I didn't promise you'd learn.' Now repeat this joke but insert *upskill* where it currently reads 'teach'. It's rubbish all of a sudden, isn't it? A nonsense word. You can make it even worse by taking out 'learn' and adding in 'your learnings'. I promised to upskill you. I didn't promise you would add it to your learnings. Sometimes it appears there is no limit to what upskilling can achieve: 'By referring to trustworthiness theories and modern software engineering methodologies, we have been implementing this program across many domains and all of our business segments. These cover the management system, culture and awareness, employee upskilling, and many others, making the impossible possible.' That is Huawei in their 2019 annual report.

Uptick. You mean increase. Saying that something has 'ticked up' is already a sign that something is the matter. Saying 'uptick' is an application to be locked up. 'A significant uptick that was predominantly driven by the channel, who is transforming with us,' said Jim Chirico, CEO of Avaya,[38] speaking English as a fourth language.

User friendly. If you have to point out that something is *user friendly*, it is probably a warning that it isn't. If it is, you can find a more elegant way of saying that people like using it.

Utilize. Use use. *Utilize* is usually utilized, as an alternative to use, when *use* has been used and the writer doesn't want to use it again. The practice is known as elegant variation and can be found many times in Henry James. There is a slightly different instance here in the John Lewis annual report where the writer clearly wants to say the food should be eaten but doesn't know how to avoid the repetition. Hence we get 'utilized' which is only ever used when we are trying to avoid another word: 'At Waitrose we set a new target that no good food will be wasted in our UK operations and we are committed to helping halve food waste by 2030 to ensure any food that is safe to eat is utilized.'

V

Visibility. 'I have no visibility on that' is a strange way to say that nobody has told you what is going on. It sounds as if you are yourself invisible. 'There was clear appetite amongst Board members to have more visibility of top executive talent,' said the NatWest 2020 annual report. What was going on? Were they all hiding?

W

Window. Usually of opportunity. This strange phrase seems to have migrated into business at the end of the 1970s, probably as an analogy with space, to which it ought to now return. It has become so flat and in most contexts there is no need to use the word *window* at all when referring to an opportunity which does perfectly good service on its own. 'Good prose is like a window pane,' said Orwell. He's wrong; it's not, but at least he is using the word well.

Wordsmith. Writers might object to the implication that they are tradesmen for words. They especially object to being told to *wordsmith* something. A blacksmith forges something and so does a writer, sometimes. A blacksmith does not blacksmith and a writer writes. There is more to this than hurt sensibility, though. The idea of a wordsmith implies the thoughts are complete, they just need to be expressed. It has been the whole point of this book to suggest that this will not be true.

Bibliography

Amis, Kinglsey, *The King's English: A Guide to Modern Usage*, HarperCollins, 1997

Amis, Martin, *Inside Story*, Jonathan Cape, 2020

Aristotle, *The Art of Rhetoric*, Penguin, 1991

Austen, Jane, *Persuasion*, Vintage, 2007

Bernoff, Josh, *Writing Without Bullshit: Boost Your Career by Saying What You Mean*, HarperCollins, 2006

Bernstein, T. M., *The Careful Writer: A Modern Guide to English Usage*, New York, 1965

Bierce, Ambrose, *Write It Right: A Little Black List of Literary Faults*, 1909

Bryson, Bill, *Mother Tongue: English and How It Got That Way*, Penguin, 1990

Bryson, Bill, *Made In America*, Penguin, 1994

Cameron, Deborah, *Verbal Hygiene*, Abingdon, Oxon, Routledge Linguistics Classics, 2012

Cicero, Marcus Tullius, *De Oratore*, Oxford University Press, 2001

Cicero, Marcus Tullius, *On Invention*, Harvard University Press, 2021

Cochrane, James, *Between You and I: A Little Book of Bad English*, Icon Books, 2003

Crystal, David, *The Fight for English: How Language Pundits Ate, Shot and Left*, Oxford University Press, 2006

Drucker, Peter, *The Rise of the Knowledge Society*, Washington, 1993

Dummett, Michael, *Grammar and Style for Examination Candidates and Others*, Gerald Duckworth & Co., 1993

Fowler, H. W., *Fowler's Modern English Usage*, 1926, 1965, 1996, Oxford University Press

Garner, Bryan, *Garner's Modern American Usage*, Oxford University Press, 2003

Gooden, Philip, *May We Borrow Your Language?*, Head of Zeus Ltd, 2018

Gowers, Sir Ernest, *Plain Words: A Guide to the Use of English*, Penguin, 2015

Gwynne, N. M., *Gwynne's Grammar: The Ultimate Introduction to Grammar and Good English*, Ebury Press, 2013

Heffer, Simon, *Simply English: An A to Z of Avoidable Errors*, Random House, 2015

Hitchings, Henry, *The Language Wars: A History of Proper English*, John Murray, 2011

Humphrys, John, *Lost For Words: The Mangling and Manipulating of the English Language*, Hodder & Stoughton, 2004

Jevons, William, *A General Mathematical Theory of Political Economy*, 1862

Kamm, Oliver, *Accidence Will Happen: The non-pedantic guide to English usage*, Weidenfeld & Nicolson, 2005

King, Stephen, *On Writing: A Memoir of the Craft*, Charles Scribner's Sons, 2000

Kohl, John R., *The Global English Style Guide: Writing Clear, Translatable Documentation for a Global Market*, SAS Institute, Inc., 2008

Lerner, Jennifer S. et al., 'Emotions and Decision Making', *Annual Review of Psychology*, Vol. 66, 2015

Martin, Stephen and Marks, Joseph, *Messengers: Who We Listen To , Who We Don't, and Why*, Random House, 2020

Orwell, George, *Nineteen Eighty-Four*, Penguin, 1949

Orwell, George, 'Politics and the English Language', in *Inside The Whale and other essays*, Penguin, 1957

Pinker, Stephen, *The Language Instinct*, HarperCollins, 1994

Pinker, Stephen, *The Sense of Style: The Thinking Person's Guide to Writing in the 21st Century*, Penguin, 2014

Pullum, G. K., 'Fifty Years of Stupid Grammar Advice', *The Chronicle of Higher Education*, 22 December 2009

Rowntree, Benjamin Seebohm, *The Human Factor in Business*, Longmans, 1921

Samuelson, Paul, *Foundations of Economic Analysis*, Harvard University Press, 1947

Strunk and White, *The Elements of Style*, Harcourt, 1920

Sword, Helen, *Stylish Academic Writing*, Harvard University Press, 2012

Taylor, Frederick Winslow, *The Principles of Scientific Management*, New York, 1911

Watson, Don, *Dictionary of Weasel Words, Contemporary Clichés, Cant & Management Jargon*, Penguin, 2004

Weiss, Edmond H., *The Elements of International English Style: A Guide to Writing Correspondence, Reports, Technical Documents, and Internet Pages for a Global Audience* , M. E. Sharpe, 2005

Williams, J. M., *Style: Towards Clarity and Grace*, University of Chicago Press, 1990

Notes

1   https://view.officeapps.live.com/op/view.
    aspx?src=https://c.s-microsoft.com/en-us/
    CMSFiles/2020_Annual_Report.docx?version=8a3ca1db-
    2de7-c0e7-d7c5-176c412a395e
2   https://www.bat.com/group/sites/UK__9D9KCY.nsf/vwPag-
    esWebLive/DOBMZDHA/$FILE/Strategy_Summary.
    pdf?openelement
3   https://www.privateequitywire.co.uk/2020/12/16/293653/
    pe-backed-arcoro-appoints-ceo
4   https://s2.q4cdn.com/299287126/files/doc_financials/2020/
    ar/2019-Annual-Report.pdf
5   https://customerthink.com/implementing-a-customer-suc-
    cess-strategy-in-post-pandemic-business/
6   https://home.barclays/investor-relations/reports-and-events/
    annual-reports/2018/
7   https://www.wsj.com/articles/elon-musk-advises-ceos-to-stop-
    wasting-time-on-powerpoint-meetings-11607470065#:~:tex-

t=%E2%80%9CIt's%20not%20some%20mysterious%20
thing,expect%20others%20will%2C

8   https://www.bt.com/bt-plc/assets/documents/
    investors/financial-reporting-and-news/annual-re-
    ports/2020/2020-bt-annual-report.pdf

9   https://www.cisco.com/c/dam/en_us/about/annual-report/
    cisco-annual-report-summary-2019.pdf

10 https://www.servicedapartmentnews.com/news/
    urban-living-news/britain-is-behind-the-curve-getting-back-
    to-work-warns-savills-boss/

11 https://www.prweek.com/article/1702631/ogilvy-names-
    julianna-richter-global-ceo-pr-influence

12 https://www.bridgemi.com/michigan-government/
    what-jennifer-granholms-appointment-energy-secre-
    tary-means-michigan

13 https://www.marketingweek.com/john-lewis-credits-bricks-
    and-clicks-success-for-decisive-market-share-gain/

14 https://www.santander.com/en/shareholders-and-investors/
    financial-and-economic-information/annual-report/2019-on-
    line-report

15 https://www.standard.co.uk/business/heineken-new-manag-
    ing-director-david-flochel-b320581.html

16 https://www-file.huawei.com/-/media/corporate/pdf/annu-
    al-report/annual_report_2019_en.pdf?la=en-gb

17 https://uk.reuters.com/article/
    us-facebook-advertising-unilev/unilever-to-resume-advertis-
    ing-on-facebook-twitter-in-u-s-idUKKBN28S06M

18 https://www.forbes.com/sites/
    jenniferleighparker/2020/05/21/expedia-ceo-goog-
    le-tried-to-disintermediate-us/

19 https://rew-online.com/ares-management-harvest-sell-valet-living-to-gi-partners/

20 https://www.reinsurancene.ws/we-must-future-proof-lloyds-says-ceo-john-neal/#:~:text=%E2%80%9CWe%20have%20to%20future%2Dproof,market%20constitu-ents%2C%E2%80%9D%20said%20Neal

21 https://www.bizjournals.com/sanfrancisco/news/2020/12/21/bay-area-bank-ceo-on-covid-s-impact-in-2021-busi.html

22 https://www.bloomberg.com/news/articles/2020-12-17/mcdonald-s-investor-group-calls-for-board-exits-over-easter-brook

23 https://www.cnbc.com/2020/12/17/will-business-trav-el-return-with-covid-vaccine-executives-are-split.html#:~:text=%E2%80%9CSocial%20experiences%2C%20like%20a%20meal,each%20other%2C%E2%80%9D%20Taneja%20said

24 https://www.personneltoday.com/hr/arcadia-group-ap-points-administrator-debenhams-buyer-talks-collapse/

25 https://www.ft.com/content/9debcf65-7556-4247-8abb-1d165391343f

26 https://interestingengineering.com/spacexs-latest-star-ship-prototype-spontaneously-falls-over-on-assembly-stand

27 https://www.bloomberg.com/news/articles/2020-12-11/apple-s-cook-says-most-staff-won-t-return-to-office-until-june

28 https://www.wired.co.uk/article/uber-coronavirus-chaos

29 https://www.expressandstar.com/news/uk-news/2020/12/23/ann-summers-creditors-approve-rent-plans/

30 https://markets.businessinsider.com/news/stocks/tesla-stock-

big-short-michael-burry-elon-musk-share-issuance-2020-12-1029859345?utm_medium=social&utm_source=facebook.com&utm_campaign=sf-bi-main&fbclid=iwar1sqccslitkgvn-qbfo3kiqscwhkaen7es8fdjxwgnpstpxpqbdzdglgxqw

31 https://www.teaandcoffee.net/news/26021/lavazza-faena-district-miami-beach-announce-multi-year-partnership/

32 https://fr.reuters.com/article/idUSKBN1XO1L2

33 https://www.mirror.co.uk/news/politics/amazon-workers-take-eight-weeks-23190262

34 https://www.cnbc.com/2020/12/11/at-least-80percent-of-office-occupancy-to-return-post-pandemic-cbre-ceo.html

35 https://finance.yahoo.com/news/goldman-sachs-ceo-on-hiring-recruiting-skill-151104203.html

36 https://www.quattrodaily.com/bentley-will-find-more-synergy-under-audi-than-porsche/

37 https://techcrunch.com/2020/06/11/facebook-chief-diversity-officer-report-sheryl-sandberg-juneteenth/

38 https://www.crn.com/news/networking/avaya-s-jim-chirico-cloud-subscriptions-far-outpacing-competition